STARTING AND RUNNING A HOLIDAY COTTAGE BUSINESS

If you want to know how ...

Book-keeping and Accounting for the Small Business
How to keep the books and maintain financial control over your business

'Compulsory reading for those starting a new business and for those already in the early stages.' – Manager, National Westminster Bank (Midlands)

Buying and Running a Guesthouse or Small Hotel
Make a fresh start and run your own guesthouse

'A thorough and practical guide and an all encompassing read, this book is suited to all those seeking a lifestyle change whether experienced or not in the hotel industry.' – Hospitality Journal

Just Six Guests
First-hand, encouraging advice on how to run a small B&B

'...guidance on conducting proper research, complying with the law, preparing the rooms, looking after guests, marketing, pricing and book-keeping.' – www.visitengland.com

Please send for a free copy of the latest catalogue:

How To Books
3 Newtec Place, Magdalen Road,
Oxford OX4 1RE, United Kingdom
email: info@howtobooks.co.uk
http://www.howtobooks.co.uk

STARTING AND RUNNING A
HOLIDAY COTTAGE
BUSINESS
An Insider Guide to setting up a successful enterprise

Gillean Sangster

howtobooks

First published by How To Books Ltd
3 Newtec Place, Magdalen Road
Oxford OX4 1RE, United Kingdom
Tel: (01865) 793806 Fax: (01865) 248780
info@howtobooks.co.uk
www.howtobooks.co.uk

British Library Cataloguing in Publication Data.
A catalogue record for this book is available from the British Library.

Cover design by Baseline Arts Ltd, Oxford
Cover photograph Phil Downey Photography, padkirk@aol.com
Illustrations by Nicki Averill
Produced for How To Books by Deer Park Productions
Typeset by PDQ Typesetting, Newcastle-under-Lyme, Staffs.
Printed and bound in Great Britain by Bell & Bain Ltd, Glasgow

NOTE: The material contained in this book is set out in good faith for general guidance and no liability can be accepted for loss or expense incurred as a result of relying in particular circumstances on statements made in the book. Laws and regulations are complex and liable to change, and readers should check the current position with the relevant authorities before making personal arrangements.

Contents

Preface   xi

1   **An Introduction**   1
    The self catering option   2
    When?   4
    Where?   5
    What?   6
    How?   6
    The plan   7

Part One: Setting up the business   9

2   **Are you Ready?**   11
    Reasons to set up a self catering business   12
    Are you the right sort of person to succeed?   16
    Your plan so far   19
    Check points   23
    Progress plan   24
    The next step   24

3   **Identifying Your Guests**   26
    Overseas tourists   27
    Walkers and climbers   28
    Families   29
    Couples   30
    Groups   31
    Weekenders   32
    Top end of the market   33
    Romantic breaks   34
    Check points   34
    Progress plan   35
    What comes next?   35

4   **Choosing Your Area**   37
    City or town living   38
    The sea   40
    In the countryside   41

Close to main attractions 44

Check points 45

Progress plan 46

Looking ahead 47

5   **Choosing Your Property** **48**

Single cottage or house 50

Apartments 51

Group of cottages 53

Large house letting 54

Chalets or lodges 55

Exclusive group of cottages 58

Check points 59

Progress plan 60

The next step 61

6   **Building and Converting** **62**

The building work 63

Planning permission 63

The properties 64

Check points 74

Progress plan 76

On to the next stage 77

7   **What You Need to Provide** **78**

The rooms 79

General equipment 84

Progress plan 85

In conclusion 85

8   **Designing, Decorating and Furnishing Your Property** **87**

Overall style 88

Taste 90

The rooms 90

Check points 96

Progress plan 97

In conclusion 98

9   **Sorting Out the Finance** **99**

The business plan 100

Cash flow 106

Grants 109
Check points 110
Progress plan 111
Moving on 111

10 The National Tourist Boards 114
England 114
Wales 115
Scotland 116
Northern Ireland 116
Quality Assurance 117
Check points 125
Progress plan 126
In conclusion 126

11 Other Quality Assurance Schemes 128
Green schemes 128
Walkers and Cyclists Welcome schemes 132
Disability schemes 135
Check points 139
Progress plan 141
In conclusion 141

12 Tourism Organisations 143
UK wide 144
England 144
Wales 147
Scotland 151
Northern Ireland 155
Progress plan 158
In conclusion 159

Part Two: Making a success of your business 161

13 Marketing and Advertising 163
Agencies 164
How to reach your visitor – an example 165
Advertising 166
Check points 176
Progress plan 178
In conclusion 178

14	**Running the Business**	**179**
	The booking form	180
	Pro-forma letters	182
	Enquiries and bookings	183
	Methods of payment	187
	Insurance	189
	Keeping guest records	190
	Simple book-keeping	191
	Check points	194
	Progress plan	196
	After the booking	197
15	**Providing the Service**	**198**
	Attitude	199
	What to provide	202
	What not to provide	206
	Questionnaires	209
	Complaints	211
	Check points	212
	Progress plan	214
	In conclusion	214
16	**Keeping Up Standards**	**215**
	Cleaning	216
	Repainting and decorating	219
	Renewing furniture, bedding etc	220
	Outside maintenance	222
	Check points	224
	Progress plan	225
	In conclusion	226
17	**Knowing the Regulations**	**227**
	Fire	228
	Utilities	230
	Health and safety	233
	Employment regulations	233
	E-commerce regulations	234
	Dealing with a death on the premises	235
	Insurance	236
	Data Protection Act	236
	Check points	237

Progress plan   237
Where do you stand?   239

18 Business Matters   **241**
Setting up an office in your home   242
Business rates   246
Tax and National Insurance   248
VAT   250
Check points   252
Progress plan   254
In conclusion   255

19 Maintaining the Momentum   **256**
Keeping yourself motivated   257
Large scale refurbishment   260
New ideas   261
Refining your market   264
Check points   270
Progress plan   272
Your future in self catering   272

Appendix   **274**

Index   **290**

Preface

When we moved to Wiltshire from London we had no plans to start a self catering business. We were downshifting from a city life, to what was intended to be a more relaxed lifestyle in the country. Certainly we knew that there was a small thatched cottage in the garden of the property we had bought, but we had no thought of what we were going to do with it. In the excitement of the move and the busy weeks that followed we more or less ignored the cottage, only checking it over for any possible problems.

Then one day when the sun was shining, we took a break from decorating and really took a close look at it. There was a small and very old kitchen downstairs with a reasonably sized sitting room. The stair rose from this sitting room to the first floor where in order to reach the only bedroom, you had to walk through the bathroom. Outside there was a small but secluded garden facing over the field beyond.

The idea then came to us. It would make a perfect letting property. It would take a considerable amount of work, a new kitchen and a new bathroom, re-sited so that the bedroom was accessible directly from the landing, but, with a great deal of hard work, the plan was possible.

Eventually it was almost ready and we approached the local tourist information office. The woman there came to inspect it, liked it, and our business was born! We had no experience before and yes, we made mistakes in the learning process, but over the next few years the business grew to give us a small but reliable income.

This early beginning in self catering made us enthusiastic to expand. When we moved to Scotland, looking to downshift even further, we were searching for a property where we could realise our dream. At Ardochy House in the West Highlands, we found it. Here we began to put into practice all the lessons we had learnt with our first small project. And with this larger venture, we are still learning.

The intention of this book is to help anyone who is thinking of starting and running a self catering business to also realise their dream. There are chapters on what to look for in a property and how to convert the buildings for use as holiday cottages. I have listed addresses and websites you might find useful for information on tourism in your area, setting up a business and dealing with official bodies of one sort or another. There are details of exactly what you need to provide for your properties in the way of equipment and furnishings and how to achieve the Quality Assurance Standard you are aspiring to. There are hints on how to present the properties for maximum effect and how to maintain the inside and the outside of the buildings. And very importantly, the book looks at the financial side of the planning and upkeep, and once you are in business, how to keep those vital bookings coming in.

Above all, I wanted to encourage anyone who is thinking about self catering as a way forward to take up the challenge. I hope that this book will give a guide to anyone in that position as to exactly what is involved in the business. We have certainly never regretted our decision and although there has been, and still is, a lot of hard work involved, we have never got over the feeling of achievement when a visitor, having been shown round a cottage on arrival, turns to us and says 'This is really lovely.'

It is still a pleasure to see guests, tired after the journey and often stressed out with working long hours, gradually relax over the next few days. It is a treat when a visitor invites you in to 'their' cottage for a drink or to discuss something and seems so very much at home there. It is satisfying to see people, who live for most of the time in a town or city, standing looking over the loch, watching the buzzards fly or listening to the call of the black throated divers.

I hope you find the ideal spot for your business and that this book will give you help and encouragement to persevere towards realising your dream.

Gillean Sangster

1

An Introduction

Leisure is an ever growing industry in Britain. People with the increasingly frenetic lifestyle of today's city living need a break from the commuting and constant pressure of the daily grind. But it is not just pressurised workers who are holidaying in this country. Foreign visitors, families, retired couples, honeymooners and groups of friends – the field is a wide one. All have their own likes and dislikes and their own very distinct requirements. Tourism is big business and accommodation for these tourists takes many forms – hotels, guest houses, bed and breakfast establishments, caravan parks, campsites and, of course, self catering.

Tourism is now a year round industry. It used to be that the main holiday of the year was a fortnight in July or August in Britain. Now, although the peak season is still July and August, it is becoming less common for people to take their whole holiday entitlement in those months and less common for that holiday to be in this country. They more often than not decide to go abroad for that main summer holiday, but then take a short break in the autumn or spring in this country.

Two-centre holidays, where visitors can enjoy the benefits of the town for a week then have a restful week in the country, are gaining in popularity too. Foreign visitors may well choose to stay in two different places in Britain, from which they can see as much of the country as possible.

The season can even stretch throughout the year depending on where you are located. Outdoor activities, city breaks and special interest holidays are popular in all seasons, while there is a growing trend to spend Christmas or New Year with family or friends, getting away from it all in the countryside.

The self catering option

More and more people, however, are interested in the self catering option on holiday. Freedom to come and go as they please, privacy, flexibility, value for money and relaxation are all popular reasons given for this preference. The self catering field is a wide one. From castles to farmhouses, from country estates to chalet parks, from boathouses to lighthouses, a self catering holiday can be a unique experience and a chance to live for a while in very different surroundings to those you are used to.

Self catering holidays can be amazingly diverse in character, suitable for all kinds of people, many of whom may not have considered them before.

◆ For families there is a wide choice of location, with extra facilities that will provide activities for the children – swimming pools, adventure playgrounds, working farms or just freedom and space to play in and have fun.

♦ For those who want more sophisticated pleasures there are apartments for holiday rental in most of the major towns and cities with all the facilities of city life on their doorstep – pubs, clubs, museums, theatres, shops and restaurants.

♦ For the outdoor enthusiast there are cottages in the mountains, on the moors or by the sea. These include specialist centres for horse riding, mountaineering, water sports or orienteering, for example.

♦ For those in search of luxury there are castles, wonderful estate houses and unique properties of a very high standard.

♦ For those who want total privacy there are remote cottages, distant lighthouses or island properties.

♦ For groups of visitors holidaying together there are large houses, castles and cottages situated close to each other.

Many more people cannot be so easily categorised but just want a holiday that gives them peace and quiet to recover from the stresses of modern day living and a space to themselves.

Self catering and you

If you are even considering running a self catering business then you are probably interested in a different lifestyle to your present one. Unlike the setting up of many bed and breakfast businesses this is a very large commitment in terms of money, property, and time. A small bed and breakfast can be run from your house with very little extra investment, but for a self catering establishment to succeed you will need to set up a certain number of distinct properties. These must be decorated and equipped to a high standard, while at the same time you will have to have somewhere to live yourself, whether you decide to live on site or at some distance.

You will probably be contemplating moving to another location to set up your business. This is a decision for all the family to make as it will be a very 'hands on' experience for everyone, including children.

Financial considerations will be among your most important decisions. Can you afford the move? You will be living for a while on a very low income while you set up the business and get it running, unless you intend the business to be a part time one. In this case, you might be looking for new and less demanding employment for the future. Or maybe one of you will continue to work in his or her present job while the other sets up the new business.

Can you afford any necessary building work and will you have a contingency fund available for those unexpected problems that are bound to arise? You will also need to decorate and furnish your properties to a sufficient standard to be acceptable by the Quality Assurance Advisor. If you are buying an existing business, are there changes you want to make to the properties? These should be budgeted for, over and above the cost of your property purchase. And of course there is the marketing and advertising. Without this no one will hear about your new business. You will need to cost in the design and setting up of a web site, advertising on other websites, newspapers, magazines and with the National Tourist Board. There is a great deal to think about.

When?

When is the right time to make the move? The quick answer is that there is no perfect time. Only you can decide when it is right for you. The very fact that you have been thinking about it seriously is a good indication that the time to make the move may be in the very near future.

If you have a young family however, this might not be wise. Running a new business takes time and commitment. Looking after a young family takes exactly the same. Can you hope to have enough time and energy for both? It might be better to wait a little until the children are older and more independent.

Maybe you have been thinking about the possibility of moving for some time and feel that it is now or never? Have you perhaps taken early retirement in order to make the move? Or are you fed up with that daily commute and want to move to the country to have more time with your partner?

Where?

Exactly where you set up your business depends on the

◆ availability of suitable property in an area;
◆ the type and size of self catering business you want to run;
◆ the cost of property (both your own and the one you want to buy);
◆ your intended lifestyle and of course, your own preferences.

The last one will probably be the one you start off with but you will have to carefully consider if your choice is acceptable to all the family and will attract sufficient visitors to that location to bring in a good income.

In this country we have an amazing variety of scenery and countryside. Even our towns and cities offer very different aspects for living – cathedral and university towns, historical or market towns and capital cities.

You may be interested in moving to the seaside with locations as varied as the south coast of England, the glorious coastline of western Wales, the picturesque fishing villages of Cornwall, Devon and Fife or the flat open stretches of the Norfolk coast.

You might prefer the countryside of Devon, Herefordshire, Wiltshire or East Anglia or perhaps you are intending to move to the remote areas of the Welsh mountains, the West Highlands of Scotland, the Dales or the Lake District.

◆ TOP TIP ◆

Wherever you choose, it has to be somewhere tourists will want to visit.

Are there many known attractions nearby or is the countryside itself enough of a draw for visitors?

What?

◆ Do you know exactly what you are looking for?

◆ Are you planning to run a large chalet park, to buy wooden lodges, traditional cottages, purpose built houses, apartments or convert a stable block or farmstead?

◆ Will you want to buy a business that is already up and running or do you intend starting from scratch?

◆ Do you want to run an additional business such as a riding school and use the letting cottages as part of the package deal?

◆ Do you want to run a business all year round or are you intending to be open only part of the year?

◆ Will you want to live at the property itself or at a distance?

◆ Are you going to convert part of the property for your own use or do you hope for a separate house?

How?

◆ How do you intend to finance the business?

◆ Will you be able to purchase the property or properties and carry out any building work with the money you will make by selling your present house or will you require any loans?

◆ Do you know what grants are available and how and where to apply for these?

You will need to know how to draw up a business plan to raise the finance for your project.

You also need to know what you have to supply to equip and furnish the properties:

You should find trade organisations you could join to get discounts on furnishings and equipment. You will also need to be aware of fire regulations, disability legislation and health and safety standards and what you need to do to comply with them.

The Plan

This book is intended to guide you through the different stages of setting up and running your new venture. The first part of the book is about preparing to enter the self catering business. It will help you identify your market and your ideal guests, where you want to establish the business and the kind of self catering you are interested in.

The book will lead you through the decisions on any building works you might have to carry out once you have chosen your property. There are chapters with guidance on how to carry out the decoration, furnishing and equipping of the cottages to meet the requirements of your visitors and of the quality assurance schemes in operation in Britain. You will also find advice about the disability regulations and the green schemes in operation in England, Scotland, Wales and Northern Ireland.

Once you have established your business you will need to run it successfully. The book gives advice on the marketing and advertising of your properties and some guidance on how to take bookings and record payments. And of course there are the visitors themselves – how do you keep them returning year after year and encourage them to tell their friends about you? How do you expand your market and meet new, possibly more demanding standards?

I hope to help you develop your own life style in the way you want to. The plan is not to move house to become stressed out meeting targets and dealing with impossible problems. You want to run a business but you also want to enjoy your new life. We have managed this and I hope that, with the help of this book, you will be able to do so too.

Part One
Setting Up the Business

2

Are You Ready?

So you want to run a self catering business. The tourism industry is a wide one, taking in many different bodies, businesses and attitudes. All these work towards providing the visitor with an excellent and memorable stay in our country. If you are to be part of this industry you will need to look carefully at visitor trends, tourist agencies, geographical locations and visitor attractions as well as accommodation requirements, quality assurance, legal responsibilities and the different regulations you will have to comply with.

If this sounds daunting – it need not be. This book will guide you through the stages of setting up a self catering business and then keep you on the right path once your business is established.

Before setting out on the path to your new life it would be wise to do some serious thinking, to ask yourself some searching questions and to plan exactly the kind of self catering establishment you want. First though – why are you interested in running a self catering business?

Reasons to set up a self catering business

There could be many different reasons for wanting to set up a self catering business and more than one of the following statements could be relevant to you.

a) You want to move into tourism and you think self catering is an easy option.

b) You have been on holiday in a cottage and it seems a pleasant way of earning a living.

c) You live in the country and need an extra income but do not fancy running a bed and breakfast. Self catering seems the next best option.

d) You know someone who is in the business and have talked at length to them about it.

e) You want to move to the country and have a less stressful lifestyle.

f) You enjoy decorating and interior décor and would find it fun setting up the cottages.

g) You have noticed an advertisement for the sale of a self catering business and it sounds tempting.

h) The children have left home and you are rattling round in a house that is too big but would give you a large sum for investment if you sold it and moved to a different area. You would still need some sort of income and see this as a good life style move.

i) You have a weekend or holiday cottage and want to let it out to visitors on occasion.

j) You have cut your teeth on letting out a single property, perhaps your holiday home, and enjoyed it enough to want to make a real business out of it.

EXERCISE

How many of these apply to you? Note which. If you have a different reason or reasons write them down for future reference

----

Any additional personal reasons:

Let's look in more detail at the list.

a) You think self catering is an easy option

If this is one of your reasons then you may not have considered all that is involved in the self catering business. It may seem that because you have, on the whole, one day a week when you are really busy with the changeover, all the rest of the time you have little to do. It depends on the size of your venture, but on the whole, this is not so. You will probably need to make a large financial commitment in starting up the business, so it is essential that you are clear about what is involved in running self catering cottages on a day-to-day basis. You could put all the responsibility in the hands of others but then this would affect your overall income as you would have to pay an employee and possibly an agency.

b) You have been to a self catering cottage and you enjoyed the holiday.

Staying in a cottage yourself, while perhaps giving you an idea of the sort of accommodation you like, is not enough of a guide to whether you will enjoy providing the experience for others. It will, however, help you realise what is needed in the way of furnishings, equipment and facilities. You have seen a self catering business from the customer side, but now you need to find out about the financial side, the regulations you will need to abide by and the marketing possibilities.

c) You live in the country and need an extra income but do not want to set up a B&B

The commitment to self catering is a very real one in terms of money, property, equipment and life style and needs serious consideration. At the very least you need to realise the difference in running the two different businesses but you still need to find out more before you make a binding decision.

If you have noted down a), b) or c) and no others, then you will need to do some hard thinking. Self catering is not an easy option unless you intend putting all the responsibility in the hands of others. Wanting to be in the tourism business, but not as a B&B, is not really enough of a response either. You need more than that. Have you noted some more positive reasons for moving into the business?

d) You have talked at length to someone in the business

If you can say 'yes' to this then you are heading in the right direction. Those in the same business are the best people to talk to. If their business has been up and running for some time they will be able to advise you on the 'ins and outs' of their strategy and give you an honest assessment of self catering as they see it. You will need to find out a lot more though. They may be running two or three cottages while you are considering a larger enterprise. They may work through an agency for bookings and you might be intending to run the whole operation yourself. They might be living at some distance from their holiday properties and you might be intending to live on site.

e) You want to have a less stressful life in the country

If you answered 'yes' to e) you could be seeing the venture as a way of living where you want and using the business to support that decision financially. Some owners of holiday accommodation could well argue that running a large chalet park is considerably more stressful than their previous employment. However lovely the countryside around them, they have little time to enjoy it. This, however, is one of the main reasons we chose to set up our own, much smaller business. We have only a few cottages and running this business leaves us plenty of time for other activities. A balance has to be maintained though, between the number of cottages and the need to make a living. Having too few cottages will mean you will need an additional source of income. With too many cottages, you could find yourself with no time to enjoy the new life you hoped for and a very large financial commitment to worry about.

f) You would find all the decorating and furnishing of the cottages fun

I certainly loved planning and carrying out the decoration of our holiday cottages but it is only a part of the business and it is important not to place too much emphasis on it alone. Choosing the furniture, picking out those smart accessories and equipping the kitchen is very enjoyable indeed. But once the cottages are decorated and the furniture is in place, you have a business to run.

g) An advertisement for a self catering cottage business looks tempting

Did you answer 'yes'? This is a good start. But there must be more than this. There would have been several other businesses for sale on that same newspaper page – cafes, restaurants, hotels, bars, B&Bs, garages, shops. Why did you choose self catering? Have you selected some of the other points a) to j) in this list as well?

h) You see this as a good business investment now that the children have left home

h) You are at least thinking financially. If you can raise the capital and see the business as a long term strategy, then this is a positive step. Are you sure that this is the right investment for you though? Have you considered other possibilities? You still may not want to be too far away from your children or your friends even though you are contemplating a move. Do you really want the responsibility of running any sort of business at all?

i) You want to let out your weekend cottage

Letting out your present family weekend cottage is a good way to start off in the self catering world. You may develop a real taste for it and want to expand your business later. If however it does not work out or you decide it is not for you, the letting side of it can be brought to a halt and you will still have the cottage for your own use.

j) You have already had some experience, now you are ready to expand

If you have any experience of letting properties then you are very much closer to guaranteed success in your new business. You are used to dealing with visitors, you know what they expect in the way of standards, equipment, furnishings etc and you still feel enthusiastic about making a business out of the concept. All very positive.

Assuming that you have good reasons for wanting to be in self catering: can you make a success of it? Have you the personality and attitude to cope with the guests and keep on top of the financial side of the business?

Are you the right sort of person to succeed?

Your main assets, after the properties, are your guests. They are the life blood of the business. Setting up all these beautifully decorated and equipped properties is only the start. You still have to attract the visitors in the first place and then make them want to return year after year, while continuing to attract new visitors as well.

You may be intending to live on site or at a distance but in either case you will need to be able to deal with people. Perhaps you have met the sort of surly holiday cottage owner who made you feel you were trespassing on their territory or that they were only in the business for the money. A holiday should be a pleasant experience for your guests and it should be a pleasure for you to provide it for them. Otherwise why are you considering it as a business? There are much easier and more lucrative ways of making a living.

It is time to be honest about your **personality**, your **attitude**, the **experience** you have, your **skills** and last but not least, the **family** and **any pets!**

Consider the following points.

- **Personality**. Do you like people? You will need to be fairly outgoing, friendly and even tempered, able to cope with people not always at their best and when you are not at your best. Are you a fairly easy going person or are you a stickler for detail? Remember that you will be taking bookings, sending out letters of confirmation, dealing with the cash flow. Although it is important to be relaxed and friendly with your visitors, you will also have to be organised and systematic with the book keeping and the money side of the venture. Are you a self motivated person? You will be self employed in your new business. It takes a great deal of self discipline to run your own business, keep records, organise your marketing and keep in touch with relevant legislation and tourism initiatives.

- **Attitude**. Will you be able to cope with difficult guests? It will help if you can keep calm with visitors who have any complaints. Are you willing to make the effort to make their stay as pleasant as possible? Are you determined to make a success of your business?

- **Experience.** Have you any sort of experience of dealing with the public in your present job? Even if you have never let holiday property before, you may have had to cope with people on a day-to-day basis. You will need to know how to approach people; how to hold a conversation and how to be friendly without being too familiar.

Do you have any expertise in dealing with staff? It will probably be necessary, at the very least, to employ cleaners for the changeover day.

◆ **Skills.** Are you a practical kind of person? Experience in DIY or painting and decorating could be helpful. Think about whether you will be able to cope with emergencies and turn your hand to most of the problems that are likely to occur about the house. Bear in mind that bringing in tradesman for small problems will be expensive and in any case, it is not always possible to find someone willing to come out at short notice. The more you can deal with yourself the better.

Do you or your partner have any computer skills? Advertising your property on the web is essential nowadays and communication by email and possibly also on-line booking facilities are essential. If you have no such skills, there are many courses available and you and your partner would be wise to take one at the outset.

◆ **Your partner and family.** If you have a partner and possibly a family, is your partner as enthusiastic as you about the new business, or at least willing to give you support and assistance? You are going to make a considerable investment in buying a property and then perhaps carry out building works. Then there will be the setting up of the separate letting properties, the decorating, the weekly changeover involving cleaning and the long-term maintenance of your new venture. Self catering does have the advantage over bed and breakfast of leaving you with a more private living space as the guests will not be staying in your house. You may not even be living on site so may not see your paying visitors very much at all. However, if your letting properties are next door to you, then your family will become involved. Are they happy to co-operate – to answer the door to requests and problems, to chat in passing to the visitors, to give advice about places to visit or directions to well known landmarks? You will all have to cope with having people walking about the garden or through the grounds at any time during the day or evening.

◆ **Your pets.** This is only a consideration if you are living in the same place as your letting properties, but if you have a dog, he or she will need to be friendly to visitors but not a nuisance to them.

Are you intending to allow pets in your properties? If so, does your dog or cat get on with other dogs or are you going to have a problem keeping them apart? Even if you do not own any animals yourself you will have to consider whether you want to allow visitors to bring pets. They can be unpopular with other visitors, especially with those who have small children who might be frightened of dogs. Then there are those guests who are asthmatic or are allergic to dog hairs.

Having said all this, it can be a considerable draw to allow dogs. There is a decreasing number of holiday properties permitting pets but we have found that there is a steady stream of visitors, even from Europe, who want to bring their dogs with them on holiday.

Your plan so far?

Before you started reading this book you will have had some idea of how you want to run your new business and the level of commitment you want to make. This may change as your ideas develop but, at the moment, how do you see the future with regard to your proposed self catering business? Just how involved in self catering do you want to be?

Do you want to...
a) Continue much as you are, without moving house or giving up your present employment, while letting one property, possibly your holiday home, as an additional source of income.

b) Buy two or three properties to let, perhaps at a distance from where you are living, and get someone to look after the business for you. Or employ a cleaner and run the business yourself from a distance.

c) Buy an established self catering business and move lock, stock and barrel.

d) Buy a house with buildings that have conversion potential for a number of holiday properties.

e) Buy a house and land and erect purpose-built letting properties.

Whichever option you choose, you will have to consider income as a top priority.

a) *Staying in your present employment while letting one cottage*

You are not really committing to a great deal. You can even try letting out the property for a while and see how matters develop. You will of course have to market the property, advertising it widely enough to secure a good rate of bookings. You will have to deal with these bookings, keep records and declare your income to the tax authorities. You may want to join the National Tourist Board in order to gain access to wider advertising and have your property inspected for quality assurance. This may mean that you will want to make improvements or add furniture and equipment in order to get the star rating you want.

b) *Run two or three cottages remotely*

Here your involvement with the business on a day-to-day basis will be minimal but your initial investment will be considerable. You may be buying properties that are already set up, which will cost more at the beginning but will make it easier and quicker to start letting them. If you are intending to adapt ordinary properties for holiday letting, then you may have alterations to make and building costs to consider. However, once up and running you can employ a manager, which will mean you have to pay a salary, or you could let the properties through an agency and employ a local cleaner you can trust.

Running a business this way means you are heavily dependent on others for success. It is a risk and it also depends how 'hands on' you want to be. You might find that there are problems you will have to solve at a distance – like getting in a plumber at short notice or your cleaner letting you down. It also means you are paying the agency and the cleaner and so make less money for yourself.

Consider whether you would be happy leaving your business to others to run. Would you want to make frequent visits to check on the condition of the properties? How far away from the properties do you intend to live? You really need to be able to reach them in a few hours if necessary.

A variation on this option would be to employ a cleaner for the changeover days but take care of the booking side of the business yourself. Then you would be able to control the financial side and arrange entry dates, but there would be no need for you to be on site unless you wanted to be. This would cut down on costs. The only downside to this is that you would have no one at the properties to deal with any possible problems. If something goes wrong with the plumbing, or the visitors in one of the properties cause trouble, you are not there to deal with it. You might need someone reliable, living in the area, to act as a reference point.

c) Buy a business already set up

At this level, you are committing yourself fully to the business. There will be a big financial outlay initially but as the business is already there, presumably with bookings in place, you can move in and start trading from the first day. You will have all the goodwill of the former business and a visitor base already set up. This can be a big advantage as starting up a new business means that you will have a period of time where you will not be making much money while you build up the business. However, buying an already up and running business may have a down side. Work out why the previous owners are selling. Have they let the business run down both in terms of the properties and the visitor numbers? Is the advertising still current? If not, you may miss a whole year in annual directories, such as the Tourist Board brochures.

You will almost certainly have your own ideas about the decoration and equipping of the facilities and the kind of guest you want to attract. This last is crucial. If these ideas are far removed from those of the former owners you may find yourself saddled with bookings from people you are not keen to encourage, while trying to build up bookings from those you want to attract.

◆ **TOP TIP** ◆

If there has been a 'pile them high sell them cheap' mentality in place and you want to bring in a more exclusive clientele, it will take time and money to establish new practices and may need remarketing from scratch.

Having said this, you may be buying a holiday business which is being run on lines you are happy with. In this case you can move in and it will be, hopefully, a seamless changeover.

d) Buy a large property and convert it

If this is your intention, then again you will have a large outlay at the beginning as well as ongoing building costs until the properties are all ready for letting.

Before you buy the property you should check with the local planning department as to whether they agree in principle to your plan for self catering. Once the place is yours, you may have to employ an architect or surveyor in order to get planning permission for the conversion and you will have to apply for a **change of use** for the property.

Doing it this way means, however, that you will be able to have exactly what you want in terms of design, subject of course to the approval of the planning department. You will be living on site while the properties are under construction, so you can keep an eye on the work going on. The downside to this is that you cannot start letting the properties until they are finished, decorated and furnished. Of course self catering is not the same as a bed and breakfast so you can start taking bookings with deposits while the work is going on provided that you are confident of the date the properties will be ready.

However confident of an end date you are, allow a margin for error – you cannot afford to have guests arriving at an unfinished property.

e) Buy land and build the business from the beginning

This is perhaps the most ambitious of all the projects. Again, before you buy the house and land, it is essential that you approach the planners to see whether they are in agreement in principle. Before you start you will have to decide on the kind of property you are going to build – traditional build, timber framed or wooden lodges. In many ways, the costing of new build is easier than that of a conversion, as the conversion may throw up all sorts of problems once you start knocking down walls.

There are so many kits on the market now for timber buildings, for example, that you will have a wide choice. Many of these can be constructed in a very short time and you could be up and running with most of the properties in a few months. Of course your guests will not want to holiday on a building site so make sure that if some building work is still continuing, it is fairly unobtrusive. Again, with this project you will finish up with exactly the properties you want in terms of number and type.

Check points

We have covered a lot of options here – and in a moment you will be focusing on the ones that you see as being important. Recap now on the key points on why you have decided on self catering as a business, whether you are the right kind of person to succeed and what your plan is.

Why?

- You have experienced holiday cottage living and the tourist industry seems to be the right one for you.

- You have talked at length to people in the know.

- You are ready to release capital on your present house and to downshift to a less stressful lifestyle.

- You own a weekend cottage and want to capitalise on it.

- You hanker after self employment and self catering seems a good option.

Are you the right sort of person?

- You are able to deal successfully with people.

- You are well organised and can keep on top of administration.

- You are a practical sort of person, who can deal with emergencies.

- You are computer literate.

- You have the support of your partner (and/or family) for the venture.

What is your plan so far?

◆ Rent any existing holiday home you have.

◆ Invest in a business and pay someone to manage it for you.

◆ Sell up and buy an existing self catering business.

◆ Convert a larger property into self catering units and a home for yourself.

◆ Start from scratch, building units on an area of land.

PROGRESS PLAN

You have been given a range of options in this chapter. Here is your opportunity to make some real choices, based on your decisions so far.

Note down your answers to the following questions.

1. Why have you decided to move into the self catering business?

----

2. What are the key skills and attributes that you will be bringing to your business?

----

3. Which investment option are you most likely to go for?

The next step

You have thought through your reasons for moving into self catering and considered whether you have the right attitude and personality to succeed in your new business. The outline plan for your business has been established and you have a good idea of how much of a commitment you want to make in terms of time, effort and money.

Now you need to move on to the next stage – the visitors. What kind of people do you feel comfortable with? Do you like the bustle and activity of lots of people around you – groups of adults or those with young families? Would you prefer the quiet life with retired couples and perhaps walkers, bird watchers or climbers? Or do you see yourself as attracting those who are in search of luxury – the top end of the visitor market?

You need to make a decision on the people you want to come to your accommodation before you choose your area and property.

3

Identifying Your Guests

Now that we have established that you have the right personality and attitude to make a success of running a self catering business, it is time to consider the next step in the planning of your future. Do you know your market? It is vital to your success as a tourism business to identify, early on, the sort of guest you are hoping to attract. You need to decide this before you choose the area you want to live in and the type of property you are looking for. The visitor who wants peace and quiet on their holiday is looking for a very different destination from those eager to experience the buzz of a city break. Climbers, walkers and outdoor enthusiasts will be looking for open countryside, while families will want a safe place for the children to play and enough in the way of activities to keep them occupied.

You have to consider yourself too. Where will you be happy? To a certain extent you will be tied by what sort of properties are on the market but it is worth waiting for one that fulfils most if not all of your criteria.

◆ **TOP TIP** ◆

The eventual design and equipping of the self catering units should be undertaken with the guest very much in mind.

You will want your visitors to return and to recommend you to their friends, so your attitude and how far you are willing to go to make their holiday special, counts for a great deal. Those extra touches matter – the design of the rooms, the information you provide, the degree of involvement you will have with your guests on a daily basis and the flexibility you offer.

Visitors fall into several types, though of course some cannot be so neatly categorised and you should be catering for more than one type in order to keep the bookings coming in. What categories of visitor do you feel comfortable with?

◆ overseas tourists;
◆ walkers and climbers;
◆ families;
◆ couples;
◆ groups;
◆ weekenders;
◆ top end of the market;
◆ romantic breaks.

Overseas tourists

Visitors from Europe often want to see as much of the country as possible during their stay. Your property will need to be in a good position for touring or close to a city that is a tourist attraction in its own right. Your advertising should mention the areas and attractions that can be reached easily from your property. If the visitors are with you for a week or more it is important that they have enough to see in the vicinity or within easy reach by car. Tourist information in several languages will help and it will be up to you to act as a source of information and assistance, particularly if any difficulties arise.

Before the overseas tourist arrives, you will need to make sure they know how to find the property and how long it will take them to reach it from their arrival point in the UK.

Official tourist information in itself is good but nothing makes up for local knowledge. It will be up to you to give them a flavour of the country on their visit. Find out if there is something you can do to make their visit special. Can you tell them about a spectacular waterfall or beauty spot or secret sandy beach known only to those in the area? Find out about farms that make cider, interesting churches, haunted houses, a village gala or Highland Games – anything that makes the visitor feel that they have had a special 'experience'.

Walkers and climbers

Places that attract the outdoor market are in open countryside, mountains, moors, lakes and rivers and close to long distance paths across the country such as the West Highland Way or the Pennine Way. There is a growing market, too, for the more extreme sports such as abseiling, white water rafting, rock climbing, paragliding etc. It goes without saying that your property needs to have easy access to the sort of countryside where these activities take place.

The outdoor enthusiast will not be spending much time during the day in their cottage. They may be less concerned about immaculate furnishings, ornaments, expensive crockery or luxury carpets. What they will need are drying rooms, good heating for colder weather, more than one bathroom with lots of hot water for when they all arrive back together cold and hungry from a long day out, and plenty of space to stow their backpacks, boots and other gear. A lockable shed or outhouse for cycles is useful too. Comfortable seating in the cottage, an open fire or stove, if possible in addition to central heating, and a good washing/drying machine are appreciated as well.

You will need to provide information about local pubs, places to eat and maps of the area. Leaflets with the 'Country Code' should be available. If you are in the Highlands of Scotland, then make sure they know about any stalking or shooting taking place round about, with indications of where not to walk in the 'season'. Provide information about where to buy fishing permits and hire boats and equipment.

Families

The family market is a large one but you must be prepared and equipped to deal with it. Not all areas and not all properties are suitable for young children.

Larger self catering establishments, with several cottages or chalets, are especially popular with families. A playground or at least a safe play area for children should be provided well away from traffic. A swimming pool, outdoor or indoor, would be a big draw but is an expensive investment, especially in the British climate. If your property is large enough, a cafe or restaurant providing family meals would be a big plus for parents who like to feel they are on holiday too.

You will have to decide on the minimum age of children you are willing to accept. For babies and very young children you will need to provide cots, highchairs and possibly stair gates. Whether you charge extra for these is up to you. The cottages or chalets should be 'child friendly' too, with not too many precious objects or expensive furnishings. Parents want to relax on their holiday and not worry about breakages or damage. This does not alter the fact that the property should be very comfortable and equipped to a high standard. Bunkbeds are acceptable for children but try to have enough bedrooms so that nobody is expected to sleep on a sofabed in the sitting room. Alternatively, restrict your numbers so that it does not happen. It is not very comfortable and the person concerned has no privacy if anyone gets up during the night or too early in the morning.

It is better to provide a bathroom with bath rather than just a shower, though to have both is a bonus. Small children and babies take baths rather than showers.

The information you provide should include child friendly pubs and restaurants in the area, and attractions for children such as seal sanctuaries, zoos and local farms that welcome visitors. Be ready with suggestions for activities such as riding, pony trekking, boating and cycling, and find out prices and times.

It is a good idea to provide games, books, CDs, videos or DVDs in the property too for the wet days.

Couples

This is an increasing market and, it has to be said, a largely trouble-free one. More and more couples are taking holiday cottages for a week or more during the year. They seem willing, too, to pay the extra and rent a four-person establishment as there are very few two-person cottages on the market. If you have one, you could find it solidly booked through the spring, summer and autumn.

Comfortable accommodation with that little bit extra in the way of luxury or special features is appreciated. Beds should be of high quality and so should bed linen and the general furnishings. If you can provide a dishwasher in the property, this will prove a popular feature. Often two couples will holiday together and it is in this situation that ensuite bathrooms are invaluable. People enjoy the company of their friends but will also enjoy a certain amount of privacy, especially first thing in the morning. This is the market that will appreciate the effort you have made, to make the cottages individual and unique.

Visitors may be interested in visiting stately homes, gardens or historic sites. They will need information, too, on restaurants and quality shops in the area, especially those stocking local goods and fresh produce, and will welcome your advice on places to visit for day trips.

Groups

There are a number of reasons why groups go on holiday together. You might well want avoid the stag or hen parties, but an extended family group getting together to celebrate a special birthday or simply to be together for a week's break is a market that can fill a large property or possibly several smaller ones. If your properties are close together or even adjoining, they can be used successfully for group visits. You will have to be prepared to spend more time at changeover sorting out all the cutlery and crockery, as groups like to eat together and this can be time-consuming to set right. It helps if one of the cottages is large enough to allow communal dining at times.

Both groups of cottages and large single houses are excellent for family parties, shooting parties, birthday or anniversary celebrations and perhaps just groups of people who seldom see each other to get together and relax. You will be especially busy at Christmas, New Year and the other main bank holidays. In the case of a large property, if you want to have the house booked at quieter times it might be a good idea to have a sliding scale of charges so as to allow bookings by smaller numbers.

Often, total luxury is not a top priority. Comfort, warmth and a relaxed attitude from you are what they are looking for. Family groups are often around the cottages more during the day, and if it is going to concern you that they are moving chairs and dishes about then do not go in for this market.

With large gatherings there may be a certain amount of noise as everyone celebrates. Again – try to be tolerant as long as it is not disturbing your other visitors. Clubs for walkers and climbers like to take accommodation together too. This is usually a quiet market with everyone out all day on the hills and moors. The same criteria apply as for the section on Walkers.

Apart from the general information leaflets provided by the Tourist Board you might think about supplying phone numbers and prices for local taxi or minibus companies. Then everyone in the group can celebrate at the local pub without having to drive themselves home.

If you have a very large property, you might also consider holding corporate events where a business or businesses take time off to hold team courses or swap ideas away from the office. It is a good idea to be able to offer the possibility of hiring staff such as a chef, maids and/or a housekeeper for the larger parties.

Weekenders

Both town and country properties are excellent for the people who like weekend breaks. There are some problems from the owner's point of view in that the usual request is for Friday, Saturday and perhaps Sunday nights. This often eats into two weeks of normal bookings from the letting point of view, especially if you are accustomed to rent your properties Saturday to Saturday. For this reason, many owners will only allow weekend letting in the quiet season. During July and August particularly, you will be hoping for weekly or even fortnightly bookings. Of course, if you have several cottages, you could accept Friday to Friday bookings in one or two, which would mean that only one week's booking would be affected by the weekend break.

Weekenders will be out to enjoy themselves in the limited time they have. They will not want to bring equipment, bedding or any of the kitchen essentials. If you have a fire or stove, consider providing all the fuel for the weekend rather than charging the visitor extra when they come. Make sure the cottage is warm and welcoming when the guests arrive in the winter months.

Let visitors know where the nearest food shops are beforehand so that they can shop on the way to the property. Have information about places to eat locally, nearby walks and any attractions within the area. It is unlikely that they will be travelling long distances once they've arrived, though they should be aware of all the possibilities.

These weekend visitors may well return for a longer holiday at some later date if they are impressed with the area and with your property. If they mention this as a possibility, show them the range of properties which might be suitable for them, especially if they say they want to bring their friends!

Top end of the market

There are certain properties in town or country which have targeted the very top of the self catering market. If you are considering aiming for this market it may be a good idea to spend a short break in one of these yourself.

It is essential that these properties are of a very high standard. Everything must be provided, from top quality bed linen to excellent equipment. Kitchens should be exceptionally well equipped and bathrooms ensuite and luxurious, perhaps with jacuzzi bath or sauna. Facilities for entertainment such as DVD and CD players, as well as the usual televisions, are required. The outside is important too. The grounds should be immaculate with a constant programme of maintenance in place.

There could be some special feature of the property which brings it into this bracket. Castles, large houses, stylish conversions of churches, chapels or barns could fall into this category, though there is no reason why a more humble cottage could not be included, provided you make sure it is of a very high standard.

For this top of the market situation, there should be no extras to pay once the visitor has arrived – no separate electricity charges, for example, and all necessities such as towels, bathmats and bedlinen should be provided.

If you are prepared to make the necessary outlay at the beginning, then this is a lucrative market as you can afford to charge a high weekly rental. However, be warned, this type of visitor can be a very demanding one and will quite rightly expect the best for their money.

Romantic breaks

A romantic break just for two in a tiny cottage at the edge of the sea or deep in the English countryside, or even in a castle in Scotland, is a lovely market to cater for. If you wish, you can choose to do this with just one of your properties, perhaps the quietest one, while carrying on your ordinary self catering business in the others.

It will not be just honeymooners who will appreciate this hideaway, but those couples wanting a special holiday on their own, perhaps to celebrate an anniversary or a birthday.

Provide a bottle of wine or even champagne if you feel extravagant. Have a vase of fresh flowers in the cottage to greet them and if you have an open fire, have it lit in the cooler months. Make everything just a little bit special and then disappear and leave them in peace!

Check points

Let's recap some of the main points of this chapter.

- Take time to identify who you see as your main guest market (with either your choice influencing the location you select or vice versa).

- Location is important – either an area with lots to do nearby or a good centre for touring.

- Different types of guests will have different priorities for the cottages – tourists might favour the homely touches while climbers and walkers will welcome drying rooms, several showers, etc.

- Family groups may favour cottage locations where there are plenty of activities available, DVDs in the cottages, etc.

- Couples – either singly or pairs of friends sharing – are a rising market, with higher level requirements such as dishwashers, ensuite bathrooms and separate living/dining rooms. These will also attract the top end of the market.

◆ The large group market, either using larger properties or combining several adjacent cottages, is another niche market. This can involve various groups, from reunions, family get-togethers, climbers/walkers etc, to stag and hen parties if you wish.

◆ You may wish to be more flexible than always insisting on weekly bookings, and consider the short break market which encourages people to have several breaks during the year.

PROGRESS PLAN

Note down your answers to the following questions.

1. Begin to focus in on your choice of key guests. Do you have a preference for type – which could influence your location – or will your selected location dictate the type of guest who is likely to visit?

----

2. Does your choice of key guests have any implications on the facilities you will have to provide in your cottages? Make a list of some of these features.

----

3. From the list on page 27, choose and write down the different kinds of guests you plan to attract and write alongside each a key marketing point you could use to attract them.

What comes next?

There are other categories of visitor you can aim for – those with disabilities or the environmentally aware visitor perhaps. These will be dealt with later as there are certain schemes run by the Tourist Boards which set comprehensive standards for these markets.

You do not have to be too dogmatic with your decision. There are older couples who are walkers or climbers, families who love the wild countryside and overseas visitors who want a romantic break. Be prepared to be flexible, but where you choose to live and the type of accommodation you buy will limit your market to a certain extent. By now you will have made the decision on the type of person you hope to attract, so consider next where you start looking for your future self catering business and exactly what sort of property to look for.

4

Choosing Your Area

You have thought about the kind of visitor you want to attract and all that this implies in terms of location. You have probably decided on how committed you want to be to the business. Now, putting these together, where would the best location be for your new property? If you are thinking about simply letting that holiday home you already have, then a decision about area will not apply to you. However, if you are intending to start up a self catering business with more than one property, you will have to decide where in the country you are going to start your new venture.

This is a decision for your heart as well as your head. What sort of area would you be happy in? You will have to tie this in with the business, of course. If you want to attract walkers and climbers, will you be happy living in a remote area away from the cities? You need to find somewhere that will satisfy you and at the same time bring the kind of visitor you want.

It should be possible to combine the two – your own preferences and the preferences of your guests. There are towns by the sea and within easy reach of open countryside. There are visitor attractions everywhere in Britain from the historic and pre-historic – castles, stately homes, hillforts and standing stones – to the present day theme parks, sealife centres and wild life parks. There are events taking place throughout the year, such as book fairs, historical re-enactments, motor cycle trials, Highland Games, boat races and food festivals. The visitors to all of these will require accommodation.

You will need to investigate your chosen area carefully in summer and out of season. After all, when the visitors have left, you will still be living there through the winter months.

You may find the area too quiet when all the visitors have gone or you may feel a sense of relief at having the place to yourself. Can you happily survive the winter there? And will you have enough to do in the off-season months?

City or town living

If you have decided to move away from a large city or built up area to a smaller town, more attractive to tourists, there is a wide range of possibilities throughout Britain. Consider:

◆ market towns such as Salisbury, Newark, Devizes and Ballycastle;

◆ cathedral cities such as Wells, Canterbury, Dornoch, Ely and Armagh;

◆ university towns such as Oxford, St Andrews, Aberystwyth, York and Durham;

◆ historic towns and cities such as Chester, Stratford-on-Avon, Edinburgh, Caerphilly and Derry.

Although you may not actually be living in the town itself, you and your visitors will be able to benefit from all the amenities available – shops, restaurants, theatres, street markets etc. How many months of the year do you want to stay open? Living close to a well known town would mean that you could attract visitors all year round. There is a large market for tourists from Europe, the USA and Canada, who want to see our cathedrals, castles and historic buildings. City breaks are popular with visitors from Britain too, especially off season in what are known as the **shoulder months** i.e. those either side of the high season. If you are also prepared to accept bookings for short breaks, then this is a good location to be in.

If the town is surrounded by lovely countryside then your visitors will have the bonus of being able to experience that too.

There is always plenty of alternative accommodation in towns and cities. You want visitors to come to you rather than the local hotel or guest house so your properties must be priced accordingly. Increasingly self catering is a family market as, for many people, it is a far cheaper option than spending several nights in a hotel. It also means a more relaxed holiday for the parents, who do not have to worry about the effect their children are having on the other guests.

There will be many local amenities for both children and adults, such as swimming pools, parks, cinemas and theatres. In times of bad weather, quite common in a British summer, there will be plenty to occupy the visitor. Transport should be good or at least better than in the country areas. Have available the name and number of a local taxi company for getting to and from the station or airport, if there is one, and home from the pub or restaurant late at night.

◆ **TOP TIP** ◆

During the quieter winter months you might consider the possibility of a long winter let.

In Wiltshire, though we did not live in a town ourselves, in the quieter months we used to let to people having major work carried out on their home or perhaps waiting to move into their new house. You could also have people coming to work in the town on a short-term basis. Putting an advertisement in the local paper could bring you a response.

The sea

Britain is an amazingly varied country and living by the sea can conjure up very different pictures to different people. From the busy resorts of the south coast to the wide, lonely beaches of the Hebrides, the sea holds a fascination for many. Building sandcastles on a sunny beach, walking along a windy shore to the sound of the crashing of the breakers or sitting high on a clifftop looking out over a perfect sea – we all have our own particular memories.

There is of course the traditional seaside image of the south coast of England, but you may well want to consider some other options as well:

◆ well-known seaside resorts such as Bournemouth, Southsea and Scarborough;

◆ the attractive fishing villages of Crail, Lynmouth, Eyemouth, etc;

◆ yachting centres such as Bosham, Brightlingsea and Cowes;

◆ bays and cliffs on the coastlines of Dorset, Cornwall, Northumberland, etc;

◆ wide open stretches of sea and sand in Wales, Norfolk, Antrim, etc;

◆ the remote coasts of the Western Highlands of Scotland, north east England and west Wales.

What kind of visitor are you planning for? Seaside resorts, though not nearly so popular nowadays, still attract families with young children and older couples who want a peaceful time by the sea with some evening entertainment. You will need to provide information on boat trips, safe swimming beaches, good walks, sealife exhibitions and, if there is still a fishing industry there, the local fish market and good seafood restaurants.

If you choose to be by the sea then it will be a real attraction if your property has a sea view. To be able to sit in a holiday cottage and gaze out over the harbour or a sandy bay will mean a lot to the visitor and hopefully bring them back to your holiday property again and again. If you are planning to attract the romantic hideaway market then a quiet cottage in the countryside by the sea will be a real draw.

Look out for old coastguard or fisher cottages. These are often beautifully situated with amazing views but remember, if you want to attract families with children, do not buy cottages perched on the clifftop or close to a coastline with a particularly rough sea.

This will probably be a seasonal market, with most of your visitors wanting to come in the summer months, particularly the weeks of the school holidays. In winter the sea can be a cold and unwelcoming prospect. Is there any way you can extend the season? Check with the local Tourist Board. There may be events planned for off-season such as a regular surfing contest or seafood festival. Tourism is an all year round activity now and many places are making real efforts to extend the season at least into the spring and autumn.

In the countryside

Living in the country is a dream for many people in Britain. The vision of getting away from it all and starting a new life somewhere less stressful continues to be a popular one. But you are going to be running a business, so to some extent the stress will travel with you. However, running a self catering business is very different from sitting at a desk all day. You will probably have no set hours of work – at least not at the beginning when you are trying to build up custom. You could be dealing with the visitors during the day then sitting down with the accounts and perhaps taking bookings in the evenings. However, when you look out of the window or wander round the different properties, hopefully you will be enjoying the lovely views around you and appreciating the sights and sounds of the countryside in a generally more relaxed atmosphere.

You may already have decided on your exact location, perhaps somewhere you have been on holiday, but before taking that final step towards purchase of your property, consider other options. It is not always possible to find a suitable property where you want to live or you might find, as we did, that larger properties are just too expensive there.

Think about:

◆ the arable and pasture lands of Hereford, Lincolnshire, Perthshire, Devon, etc;

◆ the mountains of Wales, the Lake District, Tyrone, the Scottish Highlands, etc;

◆ the hills and dales of Derbyshire, Northumberland, the Pennines, the Scottish Borders, etc;

◆ the moors of Cornwall, Devon, Scotland, North Yorkshire, etc.

Holidays in the country are always popular with both foreign visitors and those from the UK. Devon and Cornwall have been favourite destinations for the holidaymaker for years while the Lake District can almost be considered crowded in the height of the season. There are, however, lesser known corners of Britain that are slowly becoming increasingly popular with tourists.

Holidays on or near to a farm are fun for children. If you are willing to make farm life accessible to them by showing them new born lambs and calves, or providing rides in a horse and cart, for example, then they will remember it and beg their parents to bring them back again another year. You might be in cider making country or near to a shire horse centre. Is there a dairy nearby with cheese making or icecream making facilities and a visitor centre?

If you have always wanted to live on Dartmoor in Devon but cannot afford it, why not think about other moorland areas such as North Yorkshire. You will need to see the different areas in summer and if possible at other times of the year. It may save you making an expensive mistake. Countryside that looks idyllic in the summer sun can be very quiet and lonely on a cold winter day.

More remote areas

Choosing to live in the more remote areas is not necessarily the disadvantage you might expect it to be. Increasingly the boundaries of the holiday experience are being pushed ever outwards. Where once it was sufficient to have a week in a seaside resort or in the country, visitors are now becoming more demanding. Holidays with outdoor activities such as white water rafting, sail boarding, mountaineering, orienteering and abseiling are quite common. You do not have to provide all these activities, but being in close proximity to where they can be carried out is a good idea.

Then there are the very many holidaymakers who simply hanker for the absolute peace and tranquillity that these remote locations possess. They enjoy the views, the lack of vehicles, the quiet and the feeling of distance from all the hustle and bustle of their normal lives. Many of them are discovering these little known areas of Britain for the first time. They appreciate having the time to 'stand and stare' and eventually return to their ordinary lives, refreshed and invigorated. Many of them would be unwilling to live so remotely all the time but, for a small part of the year, they welcome the chance to experience broader horizons.

You may think that you would be at a disadvantage compared to those self caterers with businesses nearer to a town, particularly when it comes to getting bookings out of season – but the opposite can be true.

When we lived in Wiltshire close to Salisbury and Devizes, our bookings used to tail off in the winter months. We dealt with this by taking a long let through the quiet months. However, since moving to the Western Highlands of Scotland, we find that not only could we let the cottages several times over for Christmas and particularly New Year, but we have bookings into November and then the year starts again in February. It is mostly climbers who come in these months but we do have family parties and groups of friends at Christmas and New Year. There are those too who simply like to get away from it all and have a peaceful few days in beautiful surroundings.

The main problem in these areas is that all the usual tourist attractions, including restaurants, close down at the end of October so that those who do come to the cottages have to make their own entertainment and special meals – which they happily do.

Close to main attractions

This really deserves a separate section as it can be a terrific boost to business to be close to some well known landmark or building.

Consider:

♦ natural features – Loch Ness, Ben Nevis, Scafell, Snowdon, the Giant's Causeway, etc;

♦ man-made attractions – Alton Towers, the Eden Project, etc;

♦ film or television series areas – Glenfinnan (*Harry Potter*), Lyme Regis (*The French Lieutenant's Woman*), Glen Nevis (*Braveheart*), Loch Laggan (*Monarch of the Glen*), etc;

♦ literary venues – Thomas Hardy country in Wessex, Stratford on Avon, the Brontës' parsonage at Haworth, 'Herriot' country, etc;

♦ gardens – Stourhead, Inverewe, Tresco Abbey Gardens, etc;

♦ stately homes and castles – Castle Howard, Blenheim, Windsor, Trerice, Lacock Abbey, etc;

- pre-history sites – Stonehenge, Castlerigg, Maiden Castle, the Ring of Brodgar, etc.

Such areas are always a draw to visitors. Consider booking space for your business on a website featuring any major attraction in your area. And do not forget to feature the attraction on your own website. Using the right key words for the search engines will bring your business to the attention of the person keen to find accommodation close to their choice of destination.

Foreign visitors, weekenders, families and couples – the appeal of these sites is universal. You should have plenty of visitors once they know where you are. You should provide details of the attractions with opening hours and prices, if applicable, and feature any special deals offered by the attraction on your website. Can you provide any insights into the making of the film or series? Do you have any relevant local newspaper articles? Do you know any local ghost stories about the stately home or castle?

If you are intending to live close to natural features such as Ben Nevis, Loch Ness or Snowdon, provide weather reports for any interested climbers, timetables for boat trips and directions for your visitors to help them reach the sites.

Check points

In this chapter we have covered a wide range of areas suitable for the setting up of a self catering business. These are the key points you need to look out for in choosing a location.

- When choosing your location, take your own preferences into consideration as well as those of your prospective guests. You have to live there all year, remember!

- Visit your preferred area(s) at different times of the year, to get a sense of the lows as well as the highs.

♦ Having a property near a larger town will give facilities which can attract visitors throughout the year – or make it more likely to attract local long-term letting over the winter months.

♦ When choosing a property in a scenic area, having one which offers views of the scenery is a distinct advantage.

♦ A wide range of visitors will select a holiday cottage in the countryside. Prices vary dramatically throughout the UK, so be prepared to be flexible if a rural location is a priority for you.

♦ You can still attract visitors if your property is in a remote area. Many will seek the solitude – or come for the wild and rugged landscape.

♦ Having a property near a major tourist attraction can be a real plus. As well as giving you a focus for your advertising, it will increase the number of family bookings you will receive.

PROGRESS PLAN

You have been given a range of locations in this chapter. Here is your opportunity to make some real choices of where you will choose to live and base your business. Note down your answers to the following questions.

1. Start thinking about the sort of area you would be happy living in – by the sea, near a town etc. Would it be suitable for running your business? Can you choose an area that would combine the two?

_____

_____

2. It is time to think about more specific locations. Where in Britain could you find such an area? If it proves to be too expensive to buy a property there, are there other similar locations you would consider?

_____

_____

3. What particular marketing advantages do you think the area of your choice could provide? List as many as you can.

_____

_____

Looking ahead

By now you will have a good idea of where you want to live – by the sea, in a town, in the English shires, in the mountains. You may modify your decision once you start looking at the property available but you are probably a lot clearer about the kind of area you want to live in and the guests you hope to attract.

Even though you have narrowed the search to the sort of district you prefer – perhaps a remote area or close to a market town – there is still a wide choice available to you. Part of that choice will depend on the type of property you will be looking for – farm, chalet, manor house, manse or cottage, built in stone, brick, timber or cob. What is it to be?

5

Choosing Your Property

Britain is a very varied country when it comes to buildings. You just have to think of the black and white timbered houses of Herefordshire, the flint cottages of Wiltshire and the downlands, the red or yellow brick dwellings in the London area, the old stone buildings in areas such as Bath and the Cotswolds and the grey stone houses of Scotland.

Then there are the different architectural periods – Medieval, Tudor, Georgian, Victorian, the 30s, the 60s and the modern.

What are you looking for or do you have a fairly open mind? If you had the choice, would you prefer a farm, an old manse or vicarage, a shooting lodge, a purpose built self catering business or alternatively a piece of land with planning permission to build chalets or lodges?

Your decision depends to a large extent on exactly what you have in mind as a business.

This could be:

- single cottage;
- town apartments;
- apartments in the country;
- group of cottages;
- large house letting;
- chalets or lodges;
- exclusive group of cottages.

If you are intending to take over a holiday business that is already up and running, check whether the **good will** you are paying extra for is worth the price. You will need to see the accounts for the last few years and inspect the individual properties carefully. Is the business being run as you would run it? If not, resist paying too much extra for good will you do not need. A list of former and frequent visitors is of little value if they are not the sort of guests you will be aiming for. On the other hand if the business is going well according to the balance sheet, and the properties are attractive and welcoming, then it is very valuable to have an up and running business with visitors lined up for weeks in the future. Advertising that is currently in place is an important part of the good will you are paying for as well, as it is drawing in new guests as the arrangements for the purchase of the business are going ahead. There will have to be some negotiation, too, when you are buying the business. By the very nature of self catering, though all these visitors will have already paid their deposits, only some will have paid their final balances. Decisions will have to be made on exactly what you and the vendor receive from these deposits and balances when the sale goes through.

Single cottage or house

The range of buildings that can fall into this category is extensive: stone farm cottages, black and white timbered houses, Highland crofts, bungalows in town, new buildings of brick or wood, new timber framed houses, white painted fishers' cottages, perhaps in a row of similar houses or by themselves, estate cottages, etc.

This could be a cottage you already have, perhaps used at present as a family holiday home. Obviously in this case considerations of where and what type of building are irrelevant. If the cottage is your holiday home, you might not have been too worried about a garden or fencing for it. If you are taking holiday lets however, you should consider having the area round the cottage fenced.

◆ TOP TIP ◆

If you can make a garden or at least a private place with seating and a table, where guests can sit outside and relax and are not overlooked, so much the better.

If you are intending to build a cottage purely to let to holidaymakers, then you can make your own decisions as to style and design inside and out. Many people appreciate something a little different. When they are looking for a cottage for their holiday, first impressions count. What will they see when they look at your cottage in the tourist brochure? What is going to attract them to book with you and not with any of the other accommodation providers in your area? You will need to make your design distinctive in some way – and stand out from the rest.

If you have to buy land first then you will need to check the availability of services such as water, sewerage and electricity. Bringing these in if they are not already on-site is expensive. Do not consider buying land unless it already has outline planning permission for a house and, even then, it is necessary to check with the local planning department whether you can build for holiday letting on the site.

Is the plot of land somewhere where visitors will want to come? Does it have a view or is it close to beautiful countryside? Are there already self catering establishments in the area? If there are not too many and you are certain that you will have a market, go ahead. The very presence of the other cottages implies that there is a market. If there are no other self caters, ask yourself why not before you buy.

Apartments

Town apartments

This category can cover historic apartments, luxury purpose built flats, studio flats etc. You might think that as these apartments are in towns, architectural interest or style of building is not a factor. In many cases, however, and given the choice, guests will pick an apartment that has some special feature such as being of historic interest or in a smart new development with outlook over a river or park. If holidaying in a historic town like Edinburgh, for example, the fact that the apartment is eighteenth century or overlooking the Castle will have real significance.

New apartments in towns and cities are being developed from the former warehouses and mills, and these are often overlooking water in some form – an attractive option.

Visitors to cities are not usually expecting gardens but if there happened to be somewhere your guests could sit outside, a balcony for example, this would be an advantage.

To have a business of this type involves either buying purpose built flats or converting a building into a number of apartments suitable for holiday letting – an expensive undertaking. If you decide on the latter then, although you will not be paying quite so much for the building initially, you will have to cost the building work carefully. When buying town apartments you should also consider ease of maintenance and proximity of parking. Can your guest park close by? Is there dedicated parking for the flat?

Check whether the apartment is close to amenities such as restaurants, shops and local transport. Many visitors will prefer not to use their car once they have arrived in a town.

Is the area fairly quiet? Stand inside the apartment and listen for sound. Although you expect to hear a certain amount of traffic noise anywhere in a town, it is better if the apartment is not on a busy street where traffic will continue all through the night and where the sounds of police car or ambulance sirens may disturb your guests.

Check the proximity of railways and underground trains. While it would be useful for your visitor to have stations within a reasonable distance, it will not be so good to have the sound of trains rattling by at all hours.

The neighbourhood should be a reasonable one, with no obvious problem areas such as dark underpasses through which your visitor has to approach the building or noisy bars which will disgorge their customers late at night.

Check the conditions of purchase for any rules on sub-letting. Also, look out for any tenants' agreements which may cause a problem for holiday letting. Our daughter's flat has conditions laid down by the tenants that forbid any DIY after 6pm or at the weekend and complaints are raised if any tradesmen's vans are seen then. This wouldn't be a problem for the guests but might cause you difficulties if you were hoping to do some DIY on the flat after work some night. Check provision for taking care of the public areas such as hallways, stairs and lifts.

And where will you live? Are you intending to live nearby? You will have to buy another property for yourself in this case. You will also have to decide how much of a day-to-day involvement you want with your guests, but this is true of any self caterer.

Apartments in the countryside

There is a great attraction in staying in a large house in the country, yet having the privacy of your own 'space'. Holidaying in the wing of a castle, in the spacious rooms of a Victorian vicarage or in the elegant top floor flat of an eighteenth century manor house can be an exciting experience, far removed from most people's day-to-day life.

Castles, manses, vicarages, stable blocks, Scottish baronial mansions – the list of suitable houses is a long one. Not all of these will convert easily into apartments and if you are planning to do so you will find it very expensive. It is better, if possible, to buy an already converted property.

Are there grounds round the property? If these belong to the apartments, they are ideal for setting up facilities such as tennis courts, swimming pools or play areas if these are not already in existence. If you are not keen on providing these sorts of attractions then consider having a peaceful garden where guests can walk and sit.

Gardens and grounds will always require a lot of work. If the house has a long drive, the maintenance of this will be an ongoing problem. Flowerbeds will need weeding and bushes, flowers and trees will require constant pruning and cutting back. Are you prepared for this?

If you intend to live in the house itself and let one or two apartments in the rest of the building, then you will want some measure of privacy – can you achieve this with the property you are considering? If the grounds are to be common to all, you might think about an age restriction on any children, to prevent the sound of children playing outside disturbing the other guests.

Group of cottages

This category can consist of a group of individual cottages, a line of terraced cottages or again, individual properties spread out over an area: stone cottages, thatched cottages, coastguard cottages, fishers' houses, estate cottages, farmsteads and of course new build. The list is extensive and this is part of the charm, for overseas visitors, of holidaying in Britain. The opportunity of staying in a thatched cottage in Dorset, a stone built croft in the Scottish Highlands or picturesque Cotswold farm buildings is a big draw.

To make a living in the self catering business you would need to have more than just one or two cottages, but the exact number to make it feasible depends on your circumstances. I would suggest that if you are planning on having several cottages, then you probably want to live in the area and look after the business yourself. If you are intending to buy a ready made business, think about exactly what you are looking for. Do you want a row of adjoining cottages or would you prefer them to be separate?

If you are intending to build new cottages or convert a building or series of buildings into cottages, you have control over the style and size of the properties. New build means that you can choose the number of bedrooms and bathrooms you want and, while you are designing the interior, it should be possible to fulfil the current accessibility standards for guests with a disability in some proportion of your units.

If the cottages are widely spread out, the work at the changeover is harder and more time-consuming. If all your cottages are close to your house, it is easy to go from one to the other quickly.

Large house letting

This is a specialised market, and though other types of property do attract large parties – groups of cottages for example – this is a very good market for celebrations of any kind. Country or town manses, vicarages, former hotels, shooting lodges, Scottish estate houses, former mills, large farms, castles, manor houses, dower houses, etc in every kind of style and period – the range of these large letting properties is wide.

Many of these properties have very large rooms and heating costs can be high. You may well have original fires in many of the rooms and these are very popular with guests. Although you cannot expect to get full occupancy all year round, as these are properties which are not so easy to let, weekly charges can be high, depending on location, comfort and décor.

Think about maintenance when you are buying such a property. Getting work done on the roof is very expensive. These larger houses, sometimes hide faults which are not uncovered until later when you are having some building work done. Get a comprehensive survey carried out before purchase. Check on the heating system and on the electrical wiring. Are they antiquated or has there been some renovation and renewal over the years? What about all those corridors and rooms? Are there fire and safety measures you will need to take into account?

Large houses often have large grounds or even an estate. Check on the walls and fencing around the house – they will be extensive and you need to know if it is your responsibility to maintain them.

Where will you live? Will you be in part of this house or in a cottage or house nearby? Perhaps you do not want too much involvement with your visitors, but at least if you are close by you can keep an eye on the property. Actually being in the house itself, even if in a separate flat, might not be popular with your guests, who would like to feel they can relax as a group without you keeping a watchful eye on them.

There are particular websites and brochures for advertising this group market – take a look at some of them before you buy your property. Interior shots are revealing and you will get some idea of the standards expected.

◆ **TOP TIP** ◆

Overall you should be looking for an easily maintained house which will have good heating, and no problems in the way of rot or ancient and unsafe wiring or plumbing.

These do not come cheap!

Chalets or lodges

These can be of much the same construction – timber lodges or chalets. The style and design of timber houses is growing more exciting each year with models from Scandinavia and Germany being quite common in this country. However, many of these parks have been set up for a number of years and it would be wise to check the individual properties carefully to see whether they measure up to today's standards.

It is difficult to extend this sort of property and you will have to work with what you have. Is the insulation sufficient for winter letting? Heating is often by electricity. How efficient is it and how expensive is it to run? The conventional layout is one large room which is a sitting room, dining room and kitchen all in one, though some of the newer designs are very stylish. The property is usually of one storey – which lends itself to adaptation for complying with many of the national accessibility standards. The properties should be well set out and not showing their age too much. What star rating do they have and if you are not happy with this will it be possible to improve on it? The internal walls will in many cases be timber lined – the rooms of a fixed size. Where can you make improvements easily and without too much expense? If the furnishings are showing signs of age, replacing these can make a real difference.

There can be different categories of lodges or chalets in one park – those sleeping four, six or eight, and those of differing star ratings.

If you are considering buying a ready made business but with not quite enough income for you, check with the planning department before you put in an offer – you might well be able to build another lodge or two at a later date to extend your letting capability. Make sure this is a possibility before you buy.

If you have already bought a house with land and want to build lodges on this, again check with the planning authorities. This kind of timber building can be constructed very quickly – they often come in kit form requiring only an experienced team to assemble them. You will of course need to bring all the services to the properties, but since you already have them in position for your house, extending them should not be too expensive a job. Space them out well so that each has privacy, parking and a view, especially if it is over fields or any open countryside or onto a peaceful garden or area of lawn. Is it possible to site the buildings so that the main windows in each building do not overlook other lodges?

If you do not already have a house, where do you plan to live? If you are buying a business the vendors may be selling their house as well. Some of these businesses sell without a main house. You will need then to find separate accommodation in the area (and pay for this in addition to your letting properties) – not an easy task in more remote countryside – or live in one of the lodges. Living in one of the lodges, of course, will cut down on the number of properties available for letting and give you little privacy on a day-to-day basis.

If the business for sale has a large number of lodges or chalets, it may have extra facilities such as a laundry and reception office, with perhaps a games room and cafe or restaurant. There are sometimes swimming pools and play areas for children, boating ponds and activities for visitors to take part in such as fishing or water sports. Holiday parks can often provide enough in the way of facilities for some visitors not to feel the need to play, eat or drink elsewhere during much of their stay.

◆ TOP TIP ◆

This is not such a personalised business – you would be hard put to recognise everyone on the site at one time – but it is one of the bigger businesses and will provide you with a much larger income than that gained by simply owning a few cottages.

The letting market for these properties is a wide one and you can advertise on many fronts. This sort of holiday cottage business is also popular with the larger agencies. The letting season, however, cannot extend into the colder winter months unless the buildings are well insulated and well heated.

As this business is a large undertaking you would be wise to consider buying an up and running concern rather than attempting to buy land and build the large number of lodges necessary with all the facilities required. In some of the other categories, if you decide that self catering is not for you but you love the area, you can always sell off some of the cottages, let some of the apartments on a long-term basis or convert a large house back to a dwelling for your family. In the case of a chalet park, it can really be nothing else and you would have to sell the whole business as a going concern. If you try to sell off a group of the lodges while still running your business in the rest, you are inviting direct competition onto the site if those properties you have sold off are going to be used for a separate letting concern.

Exclusive group of cottages

This is a very high quality operation. If you intend to build one of these developments then you are looking at attracting guests from the top end of the market. Exclusive cottages or houses are often in prime locations or on sites of special interest. There are also such self catering businesses in the grounds of major hotels, next to top ranking golf courses or in remote areas of stunning beauty.

Privacy comes high on the list of requirements and all such properties should be sited away from public places and with their own grounds or gardens. Building in the grounds of an exclusive hotel means that the guests can enjoy the relaxing lifestyle of a self catering holiday yet have all the comforts of the hotel such as restaurants, leisure facilities and arranged activities for the children. Similarly for those properties adjacent to a prestige golf course guests can enjoy privileged access to the course.

There are other developments with particular characteristics. Top quality environmentally friendly houses or strikingly out of the ordinary properties such as unusual conversions of mills, barns or churches are becoming popular. The surroundings are important. Although the cottages should be easily reached by road, boat, rail or plane, they should also be somewhere that the general public has no access to: in estate grounds, on a remote area of coastline, or sheltered from view by woods and/or walls.

Tourism Boards and Enterprise Agencies look kindly on such establishments – they are perceived to raise the quality of the destination. You should be able to receive an Enterprise grant towards the building costs without too much difficulty.

If you can meet the demanding standards of your guests, you will have a top quality establishment and a flourishing all year round business.

It is not necessary for you to be living too close to this development. Your guests are unlikely to want to chat to you on a regular basis. As long as you have efficient staff and can make an appearance if called on to do so, or if, heaven forbid, anything goes wrong, this should be sufficient.

Check points

To summarise some of the important points for you to consider:

♦ Choosing your property depends largely on what you have in mind as a business. You need to decide on the approximate size and extent of your business before you begin to look for the building or buildings themselves.

♦ Running a single property business is the easiest option. In this category you will have an extensive range of buildings to choose from in all styles and periods.

♦ If you are intending to run a holiday business with apartments in town there are considerations of area, proximity to facilities such as restaurants, local transport and tenancy agreements to consider.

♦ If you are deciding on apartments in the countryside, you may have the maintenance of a driveway to consider as well as that of the grounds and/or gardens. Buying a large house in the country to convert into apartments is a very expensive option but an ideal one if you wish to use the grounds for setting up extra facilities.

♦ A group of cottages can provide a very adaptable business, as they are suitable for separate or joint letting by a group of visitors.

◆ Large house letting is a specialised market. Weekly rates are high but it is harder to fill the property all year round. There is also the consideration of where you will live yourself if the entire property is let out to a large group.

◆ A group of several chalets or lodges is ideal for the family market, especially if there are additional facilities for children on site. Again, you have the consideration of where you will have your home.

◆ Setting up a business with very exclusive and top quality cottages means that you must decorate, furnish and equip them to an excellent standard.

◆ Guests who are paying premium rates for a top of the range experience will expect quality standard and finish throughout.

PROGRESS PLAN

At this point you need to make some decisions on the type of property you will be looking for in the location of your choice.

1. There are several different possibilities to choose from the list on page 49, of the sort of self catering business you intend to run. Which of these appeal to you? If this proves too expensive or too difficult to find, have you got a second choice?

----

2. Having picked your ideal business, what style of building(s) are you looking for? This could be anything from a cob cottage to a manor house to a baronial mansion.

----

3. What special features of the property(ies) do you think would be an attraction to your visitors?

The next step

You now have a very clear idea of the kind of business you want and the area you are going to live in. You have carefully considered the sort of guest you want to attract and have made up your mind about the type of property you are looking for, whether it be large house, town apartment, country cottage or chalet park. Now it's time to move on to more detailed decisions for the future. What will you do with the building – leave it as it is, carry out a conversion or build completely from scratch?

6

Building and Converting

The design of your property both inside and out is of great importance. If you are building new properties you have a free hand, subject to planning approval. If you are putting up timber framed kit houses, then there is everything from the traditional log cabin style to an ultra modern wood and glass structure available. You will be building more than one property, so costs need to be kept as low as possible. It is important to remember that you are building to let – not for personal use – so it is wise to pick a house not only for its robust and lasting qualities and its speed of construction but also for its wide appeal.

If you are converting a building or buildings, do you want to make all your properties identical or do you want to maintain some individuality? Sometimes because of the nature of the old building, it may be difficult to make them all the same and I think that this is part of the charm of many holiday properties. We have three cottages all converted from a shooting lodge in the Highlands and each one is very different from the others. Visitors tend to grow attached to one cottage and invariably ask for a particular one when they book. It is important to give your properties names to identify them – perhaps with some reference to features in the local area.

The building work

You could be converting a large house, stable block, steading, farm building, hotel or former mill. The list of suitable properties is endless. Some of these buildings may have been used for other purposes, some may have been derelict for years and some may have been lived in until quite recently.

Alternatively, you might be considering building a property or two from scratch to use for your holiday letting. In many ways this is easier than attempting to carry out a conversion, as you start with a clean sheet. Building or conversion can be an expensive business and you may have to raise finance for it. In fact, it is usually the case that it costs up to one fifth more to convert than to build from new.

Planning permission

You will need to obtain planning permission from your local planning authority if you want to:

◆ build new premises;
◆ extend or alter existing premises;
◆ change the external appearance of the building;
◆ change a building's use (to a self catering esatablishment).

In certain circumstances you may also require listed building consent or conservation area consent. You should check with your local authority if you think this might be the case.

The local authority's planning department takes planning decisions in accordance with its development plan for the area. There are also building regulations to take into account, and building warrants to obtain if you live in Scotland.

Ask around the area for the name of a recommended surveyor or architect, as you will need to have plans drawn up to submit to the planning authority for approval. These plans will also be later sent out to builders for tendering for the contract, assuming you aren't doing all the building work yourself. Planning departments do not hurry their decisions so be prepared for a wait until approval is granted.

Details of the websites where you can find out about planning in the different parts of Britain are given in the Appendix.

The properties

When considering your building work think about the following points:

+ number of units or cottages;
+ number of bedrooms in each;
+ number of bathrooms;
+ size of the rooms;
+ direct, private access to each property;
+ layout of rooms;
+ ventilation of bathrooms, shower rooms and kitchens;
+ access to cottages from road and parking;
+ views from cottages;
+ individual gardens or outside space;
+ heating and hot water;
+ fire proofing;
+ sound proofing;
+ damp proofing;

- ◆ disability legislation;
- ◆ outside lighting.

Number of units or cottages

There is a great temptation to fit as many units as possible into the property you are converting. This is unwise. I have seen properties where the conversion has packed so many separate units side by side into the available space that the interior of each cottage has a corridor-like feel to it. The front hall leads directly to a space with an occasional bed under the staircase, then a small dining area and finally a sitting area, all in a long line. However well you furnish such a cottage it will never feel spacious.

◆ TOP TIP ◆

If you want a quality business, plan accordingly. People do not like to be crowded into small spaces even on holiday.

Even four people in such a cottage will get on each other's nerves by the end of a week of rainy weather.

Work out how many you want each cottage to sleep. Generally the number of units will not then be a difficult decision – walking round the whole building will give you an idea of how well it can be converted into the separate properties.

If you are starting with a new build, then how many cottages do you have room for on the site? Can you run a business with this number? Again do not try to pack too many into the ground available.

Number of bedrooms in each

Holiday cottages that sleep two people are rare and very popular but do not command high prices unless at the top end of the market. The more usual size of cottage is one sleeping four or six. This is because it is suitable for most people including couples who are willing to pay that little bit more to get the extra space. Those properties sleeping eight, ten or more can cater for larger families and groups. You would be wise always to restrict the number of guests in the cottages to the number of beds available, rather than allowing an extra person to spend the night in a sleeping bag on the floor. This can create pressure on the facilities in the cottage and cause problems with the quantity of dishes and cutlery you have provided.

Bedrooms are classed as **double**, **family**, **twin** and **single**. There are also those with bunk beds – fun for the children but not so popular with older adults. A family bedroom will usually have a double and a single bed. This means the room can be used for a couple with a small child or two adults who prefer not to share a bed. Bedrooms sleeping any more than three people are not recommended – it is a quality cottage and not a hostel you are letting.

A downstairs bedroom can be an asset. Elderly guests or those with mobility problems find stairs difficult and welcome this facility.

Number of bathrooms

It would be wonderful if you could have ensuite bathrooms or shower rooms. This is not always possible, however, and the official recommendation is that if you are sleeping more than six people you will need to provide a bathroom and a separate toilet – ideally in addition to the toilet in the bathroom. I am going to stick my neck out here and recommend an extra bathroom, if you can provide it, for those cottages that sleep six people as well.

Ensuite bathrooms are more and more popular in bed and breakfast establishments and I do not think it will be long before they are asked for in some of the more expensive holiday cottages. We are lucky enough to have ensuite facilities in two of our cottages – this is because the property we converted was a hotel with these facilities already in place.

We have noticed that more and more guests choose these cottages specifically because of the bathrooms – especially when there are two couples sharing.

Size of rooms

The ideal here is to make them spacious without wasting space. In some cottages the main room has both a sitting and a dining area and sometimes a kitchen area too. This room has to be spacious so guests do not feel cramped – after all they are spending most of their time here relaxing, socialising, cooking and eating. Think about the furniture you will need and build in enough space for it. If you are able to have separate sitting rooms and kitchens, then so much the better.

If you intend to have a separate kitchen, make sure your guests will be able to move around, open drawers and cupboards easily and stand at the cooker without being in the way of opening fridge doors, etc.

Bathrooms do not need to be large but they need to be well equipped. Can you fit in a bath and/or shower, toilet, wash hand basin and possibly even a bidet? There are certain minimum areas all these facilities require under building regulations – check with your architect or surveyor.

Each of the bedrooms should have enough space to let the visitor move around and open drawers and cupboards easily. Double beds should not be placed against a wall so that access is restricted to one side only. Leave enough wall space for the size of bed you are planning in addition to radiators, a chest of drawers and a wardrobe (unless you are constructing built in cupboards).

Direct, private access to each property

Can you build the properties so that each has direct access to the outside? This is easy when the cottages are individual buildings but harder when you are converting a large house or hotel. When we were looking for our ideal property we wanted one that would lend itself easily to conversion 'along the way' rather than 'up the way'. In other words we wanted a house that was long in shape but only two storeys high. We could then divide it easily into two-storey dwellings each with a front door to the outside – giving us a terrace of cottages rather than the option of flats in a main building, which is an entirely different concept.

If you are converting a large house into apartments it is probably impossible to give each direct access to the outside, but in this case you should have a fair sized communal hallway from which each apartment has access through their own front door.

The front doors in all cases should have good draught excluders and, especially if in an internal hallway, be solid doors without glass panels to maintain privacy for guests and for security reasons.

Layout of rooms

The room layout of a holiday cottage need not be the same as you might expect in a normal house. Kitchens do not need to have a back door leading out of them and there can be anomalies in the construction of these cottages which are perfectly acceptable. There are holiday cottages where all the bedrooms and the bathroom lead out of the main living/dining room. In many letting properties too the kitchen is simply in an area of the main large living/dining room. This is acceptable for most people as they are probably only going to be there for a week.

What is less acceptable is the arrangement where the only way into a bedroom is through another. Although this is fine for families with small children, it is not really an option for anyone else and will severely curtail the letting potential of the property. The necessity for any visit to the bathroom to be through someone's else's bedroom is going to be very unpopular in the middle of the night.

If you are thinking of installing ensuite bathrooms, you will have to take into consideration the guests staying in the other rooms and possible visitors to the property during their stay. By its very nature, an ensuite bathroom is for use only by the occupants of that particular bedroom. A three-bedroomed cottage with two ensuite bathrooms is not a viable proposition without a third bathroom as well.

Ventilation of bathrooms/shower rooms/kitchens

If your bathroom or shower room has an opening window so much the better, but whether it does or not it is essential that a fan is installed to comply with building regulations. Long showers or baths can leave a very steamy atmosphere which can cause mould.

Kitchens, too, should always have a fan, vented to the outside to comply with building regulations.

Access to cottages from road and parking

All the properties should be easily accessible from the road, even though it may be up a long driveway. If possible, the access to any cottage should not mean passing in front of the main windows of another. The way to each cottage should be clear and well marked so that guests can easily find their accommodation.

There should also be sufficient space to park one car close to the cottage. If the parking has to be at a slight distance then allow the guests to bring the car as close to the door of their property as possible to unload and load their luggage at the beginning and end of the holiday.

Views from properties

It is of course not always possible to have views of the surrounding countryside from your properties, but if it is, make every attempt to position any cottages you are building so that each has some open aspect. When visitors look out of their windows or sit outside, they will really appreciate this. It is a strong marketing point too.

The same reasoning applies to apartments. If they are in town then it is far nicer to look out on a park, river or even a quiet street than to overlook the wall of the next door building. Look out for this when considering properties – it is a marketing plus.

Individual gardens or outside space

Can you provide a garden of some sort for each cottage or at least a patio to sit out on? These should be fenced if possible if you allow dogs into your properties. The garden should be easily kept if you do not want to make extra work for yourself. Lawns and flowerbeds with shrubs need less attention and can be tidied up more quickly than planting a herbaceous border, which will require weeding and replanting from time to time.

Barbeques are very popular. If you are providing this facility for the cottages you will need to find an area for the visitors in each property to use them, either as a private space for individual cottages or as a general barbeque site they can all use.

Apartments in a country house may have a private or communal garden for guests to use, or if in town, a balcony to sit out on. Again shrubs, lawns and trees are ideal for the country house garden but there is not a lot you can do for the town apartment. It is risky to provide houseplants as there is no guarantee that the visitor will water them.

Heating and hot water – separate or shared

Heating and hot water for the properties will be by gas, electricity or oil. If you have terraced cottages or several apartments in a house you will have to decide whether the heating and hot water system is to be shared. A hot water tank and a central heating boiler for each property is the obvious answer, but if you have a couple of cottages together, for example, it is possible to cut down on installation costs and have one large tank and boiler for the two, with the heating zoned separately.

Will you have an AGA or Rayburn in the kitchen, providing cooking facilities as well as hot water and possibly heating? These are enormously expensive to buy and install and not many people are used to cooking on them. They can be rather off-putting for guests who are not accustomed to them.

Do you intend to have open fires or stoves? These are very popular indeed in country areas and some visitors make a point of asking for them in the cooler months, particularly at Christmas and New Year. They should be used in addition to central heating and not as an alternative. It is an extra chore to clean them out at the end of a holiday and the ashes can cause a mess, but the pleasure visitors get from them is gratifying. They also provide a good focal point for the sitting room.

Is the heating to be fully controllable by each cottage? In this case you might want to install coin meters or use a system of reading the meter at the beginning and end of each visitor's holiday. This is not applicable if you are using oil fired central heating of course. There are disadvantages to both these systems. With the coin operated system guests can be irritated by the necessity to constantly 'feed the meter'. On the other hand, when we had a cottage in Wiltshire we charged for electricity by meter reading but found that it created an atmosphere of concern at the end of the holiday while the visitor waited anxiously to hear how much he or she owed, however much you reassured them in advance that the cost would be relatively low.

In some self catering properties the heating and hot water are included in the weekly rental cost. The owners then raise the basic weekly cost to a figure that will cover the bills. Unfortunately, by the very nature of self catering, prices for winter letting are lower than summer. This means that you are charging lower prices for a period of time when you are using more fuel. If the heating and hot water are fully controllable by the guests then, unfortunately, there are always those who abuse the system.

Here in Scotland we heat our properties by oil as there is no gas in the area. Our method of compromise is to have the heating and water controls in our own house. We set them both on a timer (with differing lengths of time for each season) but make sure visitors know that they can ask us if they want the heating on longer than the set times.

Whatever the system you choose, guests should still be able to control the temperature in their property with valves on each radiator.

Fire proofing

In all properties fire regulations and health and safety rulings will have to be taken into consideration in some way. If you are converting a large house into apartments you will probably need to think about erecting outside staircases as fire escapes. Check with the planning department and the local fire service.

If you are converting a building into separate holiday cottages, each with direct access to the outside, it is as well to avoid having a room from one cottage directly above or below a room from the next door cottage. If the property is such that the bathroom of cottage A lies directly above a bedroom in cottage B, then the firewall would have to be constructed down the end wall of the bathroom, back along under the floor of that bathroom and down the end wall of the room in cottage B below. This is an expensive solution. Better, if possible, to bring the downstairs bedroom in cottage B into cottage A, then a simple vertical firewall can be erected to divide the properties.

Sound proofing

This is really only of concern if the properties are adjoining or are apartments. It could be that the building of an adequate firewall will mean that the properties are well soundproofed. As these are holiday properties and not permanent dwellings, you might think that soundproofing is not necessary. If you can install it fairly inexpensively though, it is worth doing. People are more relaxed on holiday and are there to have a good time. This means that a certain amount of noise is unavoidable but you do not want it to annoy the guests in the cottage next door.

When converting the building, consider the possibility of positioning the rooms so that the sitting rooms of different cottages are not adjoining. This will cut down on the sound of loud music or the television annoying the people in the next property. If you can place a kitchen or hallway adjoining next door's sitting room, so much the better.

Damp proofing

Damp proofing is necessary in most residential buildings. There are various companies that will install it – these are in the *Yellow Pages*.

If you are creating a solid floor it is always necessary to put in a dampproof course under the concrete. In some properties you might be lucky enough to have the original flagstones. To fully install damp proofing you would have to have these lifted and a waterproof membrane laid, before replacing them. This can be very difficult to do without damaging the stones. It is possible, however, if the property is very dry, to leave the flagstones *in situ* and use rugs. This allows the floor to breathe. Fitted carpets cannot be laid over this type of floor without a damp course underneath as the carpets will go mouldy. Why would you want to cover the flagstones anyway – they are a feature in their own right!

Private water supplies/sewerage

If the property you are converting has its own sewerage system or water supply, it might not be adequate for the influx of people you are planning. Have it checked in advance.

A septic tank is a good system to have. It will cause very few problems and only require emptying every three years or so. Modern septic tanks come ready made and look rather like giant onions with the stalk left on. They are buried in the ground, with the manhole cover at the top of the neck and should be installed below or on a lower level than your property for obvious reasons!

They operate using a gradual filtered purification process, either directly by membrane or through a sequence of tanks or subsidiary pipes in bigger systems. Emptying them takes only an hour or so and is carried out by a specialist company or by the local council.

Having a private water supply can cause problems at times, especially when the weather has been very dry for a period of time or when the ground is freezing. With the cost of mains water for business premises, however, there is a plus side! The tanks can be fed naturally by streams, or the supply may come from underground aquifers.

The only work necessary is to keep an eye on the supply and to keep filters and pumps clear. This is not arduous, especially when you realise that you are not paying water rates!

As you are dealing with the public, the supply must be tested every year for purity. You will need to install an ultra-violet disinfector, with filter, which will zap any bacteria passing through the pipework. The water is very pure as no chemicals are used at all.

Disability legislation

The Disability Discrimination Act will play a part if you are setting up any business. Your new properties should comply with this Act though a certain amount of leeway is permitted if the building is old or of historic interest. You must make every 'reasonable' effort to adapt your properties to be suitable for guests who have any form of disability.

If you are applying for planning permission to set up your self catering business, the planning authority will almost certainly make it a condition that one property at least should be set up for use by those who have impaired mobility. This means installing special facilities in the bathrooms and possibly in the kitchen. It will also involve having a downstairs, accessible bedroom with sufficient space for a wheelchair user. There are many other measures you can take to adapt your cottages for those who have a disability of some sort. See Chapter 11 for suggestions of how to respond to some of these.

Outside lighting

In country areas particularly, outside lighting is essential. There is often nothing else as there are no street lights and, with daylight fading at about 4 pm in midwinter in Scotland, the car parking area and the paths to the cottages could be plunged in gloom at a time when your visitors would be returning from a day out.

Installing a light outside the front door of each property, to be controlled from the properties themselves, will help the visitors to see their way, while good PIR lights on the driveway or car parking area, activated by movement from cars or people, are really necessary.

Check points

To summarise the important points made in this chapter:

◆ Whether you are building from scratch or converting a property into a self catering business, you need to approach the planning authorities before you buy the land or the building to make sure that they will consider the proposition favourably.

◆ The plans for the building or major conversion should be drawn up by an architect or suitably qualified surveyor who can submit them to the planning authorities for approval once the land or property is yours.

◆ It is important not to crowd too many properties onto the land or into the converted building. This will detract from the quality of the cottages and give them less appeal in the eyes of the visitor.

◆ The majority of holiday properties sleep four or six people. These are still attractive to couples who are often willing to pay the extra for the space it gives them.

◆ If it is possible to install more than one bathroom in a property, this will be a very positive marketing point. Visitors are increasingly expecting more and more in the way of facilities, and ensuite bathrooms are an additional attraction.

◆ Rooms should be as spacious as possible with no awkward angles. It is important to allow space for opening cupboard doors and for the furniture in the rooms to be positioned to allow for free movement around the room.

◆ The layout of the rooms in each property need not be as you might expect them in a private house, but there should be no anomalies such as bedrooms leading through to other bedrooms.

◆ Good ventilation, incorporating an electric fan, is essential in kitchens, bathrooms and shower rooms, to comply with building regulations.

◆ It is important that guests can park close to their cottage or at least be able to bring their cars close, to unload and load at the beginning and end of the holiday.

◆ Cottages should be sited, if possible, so that each has a clear view of the garden or countryside from the main windows. Try to avoid the situation where one cottage directly faces another.

◆ If at all possible, each property should have a private area of garden or patio, solely for use by the guests in that cottage.

◆ You will have to decide early on in the building programme whether to heat the properties by gas, electricity or oil and how you are going to charge for the fuel.

◆ In constructing your properties you will need to put up fire walls and sound proofing if the properties are adjoining. This is important both for fire regulations and the peace of the other guests.

◆ A private water supply and sewerage system need not be a daunting prospect as neither is complex to install nor difficult to run.

◆ Outside lighting is essential in country areas, particularly where there is no street lighting. Good PIR lighting for parking areas and driveways, activated by the movement of cars and people, is economical to run.

PROGRESS PLAN

If you are not buying an already existing business, there are some important decisions to make here as to whether you will want to build new properties or convert an older one. Even if you intend buying an existing business you may want to expand at some time.

1. Having decided in the last chapter the sort of self catering business you want to run, will you be looking for a piece of land or an older building to convert? How many properties do you intend to run on the site?

----

2. It is time to start planning the size and extent of your cottages. Will you have different sizes of cottage? How many people will they each sleep? List the most important factors for you – separate kitchens and sitting rooms, ensuite bathrooms, type of heating, size of rooms, etc. Will this vary from cottage to cottage?

----

3. What about the outside? Will you have gardens or patio areas? Draw up a rough plan showing the position of the cottages relative to each other, trying to give each property some measure of privacy.

On to the next stage

Now that you have established the style of the properties and planned any conversion you need to do, or indeed any new building work that is required for your business, you are well on the way to the stage where you will be making some decisions about design and décor for your self catering properties.

7

What You Need to Provide

Whether your holiday property is for two, three, four people or more, in the country or the town, stone or timber built, there are certain basic requirements that you should provide for your guests. The Quality Assurance schemes set standards that should be met for the differing levels and it is your decision as to which 'star' level you are aiming for. However, whatever you decide, for your business to succeed there are obvious necessary facilities, furniture and fittings you will want to provide.

In addition to these you will want to furnish and equip your rooms with more than is strictly necessary. You want to make your holiday accommodation inviting, attractive and comfortable – somewhere that your visitors can relax and enjoy themselves and somewhere they will want to return to for another holiday in the future. The following list is not definitive – you will want to add to and adapt it for your own properties – but it will give you an idea of what is considered necessary.

The rooms

For the maximum number of visitors to the property you should provide the following.

Sitting room/dining room

◆ A large enough table and sufficient dining chairs, with tablemats for everyone and for the serving dishes.

◆ Comfortable seating – sofa and/or arm chairs. There are several companies, mostly in Wales, which provide mail order sofas and chairs at very reasonable prices. Their advertisements can be seen in the back of home and garden magazines and in sections of the Sunday papers. When choosing your chairs, consider those with loose covers, especially washable ones. It is both economical and practical to buy extra sets of these covers and change them when necessary. The companies selling this furniture may suggest a fabric protector with guarantee, but the guarantee they supply is not valid for business use so there seems little point in paying extra for the process to be done. Provide some loose cushions for extra comfort.

◆ Colour TV (unless in an area where there is no reception – this should be stated in advance). If you have installed satellite or cable TV inform your visitors as to which channels are available. You might consider also providing a video or DVD player and a CD player.

◆ For a stove or open fire – fireguard, poker, brush, tongs, shovel, coal hod or log basket, ash bucket. A starter pack of coal and logs.

◆ Carpet and/or rugs.

◆ Coffee table or occasional tables.

◆ Extra furniture such as a dresser or sideboard to hold books, games and tourist information.

◆ Curtains or blinds on all the windows.

◆ Non-flammable waste bin.

◆ Table lamps in addition to main light.

◆ Pictures on the walls.

◆ Shades for all the lights.

Bedrooms

◆ Beds – double (6′3″ by 4′6″/190 by 137 cm), single (6′3″ by 3′/190 by 90 cm), child (6′ by 2′6″/183 by 76cm). Five-foot wide beds (British kingsize) instead of double, are increasingly popular and I would recommend these.

It is possible to buy twin beds that can zip together for use as a double. These are available either 2′6″ or 3′ wide. You would have to provide bed linen of a suitable size, for the 6′ bed, of course, but it does make a room very much more adaptable.

Mattresses should be good quality and in sound condition. Contract mattresses have a firm edge to prevent sagging when guests sit on them. All mattresses should be sprung or good quality foam. If you provide duvets, you should have a sufficient tog rating for the winter months and a lighter weight for the summer. Duvets and pillows (two per person) made from a good artificial fibre are best, both because they are washable and because there are so many people with allergies nowadays. It is also possible to buy non-allergenic duvets and pillows. If you provide blankets there should be enough for the cooler months. They should be the right size for the beds.

Use mattress covers and pillow covers – provide waterproof mattress covers or sheets for small children.

If you are also providing bed linen, nylon is unacceptable. Polycotton or cotton sheets, duvet covers and pillowslips are necessary.

◆ Carpets and rugs. If you are not having fitted carpets then bedside rugs are essential. Even if you are, extra bedside rugs are a comfortable touch.

- Dressing table or chest with mirror.

- Bedside tables or units with lamps. For twin beds it is sufficient to have a shared table/unit and lamp.

- Wardrobe or fitted cupboard with hanging space and sufficient hangers for the number of people occupying the room (six per person).

- Chest of drawers or drawer or shelf space in a cupboard.

- Curtains that will keep out the light.

- Non-flammable waste bin.

- Pictures on the walls.

- Chair or chairs for clothes at night.

- Ceiling light with shade.

Bathrooms

- Bath and/or shower with non-slip mat if necessary. A shower screen looks better than a shower curtain and is easier to keep clean.

- Towel rail. A heated towel rail is useful – and also serves to heat the bathroom.

- Washbasin with mirror.

- Shaver point with light.

- WC with toilet paper holder, brush and covered waste bin.

- Bolt or lock on door.

- Bathmat.

- Towels if you provide them.

- A light with shade.

Kitchen

- Cooker with oven (with at least two shelves), grill and at least three rings. If you want to upgrade your property, then consider a cooker with a double oven or a ceramic hob.

◆ Refrigerator with ice tray.

◆ Freezer or proper freezer compartment in the fridge.

◆ Washing machine (a washer/dryer or separate washing machine and dryer is very nice to have).

◆ Dishwasher (not necessary but very welcome if your property sleeps more than four).

◆ Vegetable rack (again not necessary but useful).

◆ Sink, draining board and drying rack with washing up liquid and dish cloths/brush.

◆ Waste bin (large).

◆ Microwave.

◆ Toaster.

◆ Cafetière or other coffee making facility.

◆ Blind or curtains.

◆ Light with shade.

◆ Fire extinguisher.

◆ Fire blanket.

◆ Cupboards for food storage.

◆ Ample working surface.

◆ Other kitchen equipment as follows:
ashtrays (if smoking is permitted in the property)
breadbin
dish cleaning cloths
sieve
cutlery box or divided drawer
tea towels
clothes pegs
breadboard and knife
chopping board(s)

electric kettle

oven mitt

tray

washing up bowl with brush, cloth and sponge

air tight biscuit/cake tin

butter dish

pepper and salt set

mixing bowl

jugs – milk, water, measuring

sugar basin

teapot

tea strainer

toast rack

knives – bread, carving, vegetable

corkscrew/bottle opener

kitchen set with fish slice/masher/ladle/draining spoon, etc.

grater

scissors

potato peeler

whisk

wooden spoons

baking tray

casserole dish and lid

tin opener

colander

frying pan (perhaps two)

saucepans – very large, large, medium and small

oven roasting tray

pie dish.

◆ Cutlery for the number of people in the property:
knives (table and dessert)
forks (table and dessert)
spoons (soup and pudding)
teaspoons (extra if possible)
tablespoons for serving (at least four).

◆ Dishes and glasses for the number of people in the property:
dinner plates
side plates
teacups and saucers
mugs
cereal or soup bowls
serving/vegetable dishes
egg cups
tall glasses
short glasses
wine glasses (red and white if possible).

General equipment

◆ Cleaning equipment such as:
broom
cloths
bucket
cleaning creams, etc
duster
dustpan and brush
floor mop
vacuum cleaner;

◆ spare light bulbs;

◆ door mat;

◆ torch;

◆ ironing board and iron;

◆ clothes rack;

◆ garden furniture if appropriate.

PROGRESS PLAN

If you have decided to start a self catering business you will probably have spent a holiday in a self catering cottage yourself at some time. Perhaps the cottage was superbly equipped and you found it lacked for nothing. Or perhaps there were occasions when you missed certain items of equipment you were used to, particularly in the kitchen. Or, were there things that were missing in the sitting room, for example, that would really have improved your holiday and made it special?

Using your experience as a visitor, note down any items which you felt were missing under the following headings:

1. The kitchen:

----

2. The sitting room:

----

3. The bedroom:

In conclusion

It may seem a daunting list of goods and equipment that you will have to provide for each property, but if you look round your own living room or kitchen you will actually see that you have much more than this. Many of these items will need replacement at intervals. Cutlery disappears, dishes are broken, machinery breaks down and carpets stain irretrievably.

◆ TOP TIP ◆

I would still advise buying good quality items. They look better, last longer and keep their shape!

I usually try to wait for the sales to buy the best quality goods. There are some excellent bargains to be had at these times of the year. If you have a large number of holiday properties, however, and need large numbers of everything, there are the specialist suppliers to the trade. These companies provide a good service if you can find them. Some of the self catering associations might be able to help with the names of suitable companies in your own areas.

I do find that it is a very important to provide as much as possible in the kitchen. At home, like everyone, I am used to using particular knives for particular cutting jobs. I therefore try to provide not just one or two knives but a selection to choose from. There are many different sized knife sets on the market – pay a little extra to get a set which keep their sharpness. You will have your own preferences, but try to see it from the visitor's point of view as much as possible and provide what you think they will want.

8

Designing, Decorating and Furnishing Your Property

This is an area where you can use your imagination and flair for colour and design while keeping firmly in mind the needs of your guests. You may have bought an existing business and have no need to convert buildings or redesign layouts, but at some stage of your business life you will need to refurbish rooms and change décor and furniture. It is in this area that you can have a little fun. You can experiment with colours that you have not considered in your own home. It is no more expensive to paint a kitchen pale yellow to bring sunshine into the room than to paint it magnolia. But whether you follow established ideas or go wild with colour – remember that your visitors have to live there for a week at a time and you want them to return!

Practicality is important. Your guests will not look after the property as you would – small children do not always behave themselves as you might expect and you could find yourself with some fast repair work to be done at changeover day. There is also the wear and tear of normal living. Walls become marked, doors scuffed and furniture stained. You do not want to have to constantly replace items either, so think and plan carefully before you begin work on the decoration of your property.

Overall style

You only have to look at one of the many house and garden magazines to see the vast proliferation of styles of decorating and furnishing. From the totally minimal to the country house chintz or French Provencal, there are so many to choose from and adapt. The area your property is in may influence your decision or you may simply have a desire to experiment. In your property you can practise with colours and designs you have never used up until now.

◆ TOP TIP ◆

Many of the more interesting hotels have rooms where the style is individual – the Japanese, the colonial, the boudoir, etc. Even if you do not want to be quite so extreme as this, you can have fun with design.

Perhaps you have a particular item of furniture, a set of pictures you have bought for the walls, or even just bedlinen with a striking pattern that can act as a starting point for your scheme.

On the other hand, it may be that you just want to paint and furnish the cottages with no fuss or bother, in a straightforward way. There is nothing wrong with this. It is simple to do and easy to maintain. However, even doing this you can incorporate some feature that your visitors will remember. We have a large sitting room in one cottage that faces east and so is rather dark anytime after midday. We could have painted it in a pale colour in order to brighten it but we chose to do the opposite. The walls are now red, the carpet and curtains patterned in red and dark blue. We furnished it with a leather chesterfield, some chairs upholstered in dark blue and good lighting. With its Victorian open fire and a mirror over the mantelshelf it is a wonderful room in the evenings and guests certainly remember it. This is a very popular cottage so we must be doing something right!

Many cottages are furnished with new pine furniture. This looks clean, bright and attractive and is available in either a modern or 'Victorian' style. There is a large number of shops selling pine beds, chests, tables, chairs, etc., so there are many different styles available. It goes with most colours and is a wood which is universally popular.

Then there is the distressed style of furniture, perhaps more suited to the Mediterranean countries, reproduction and the genuine antique. The word 'antique' covers furniture of the Victorian period which is readily available in sale rooms and at auction, though you would not consider putting the more valuable antique furniture into holiday cottages. Some of the heavier Victorian pieces are ideal for older properties though they would not suit a timber lodge or chalet.

A minimalist look is hard to achieve successfully in a holiday cottage without the whole place looking bare and uninviting. With no personal possessions around to soften the hard edges, it is not a style I would recommend.

There are also other very distinctive 'themes' of furniture or furnishings such as that of Rennie Mackintosh, the Glasgow architect and artist, or, more up to date, those of Laura Ashley and Sanderson.

If you have a large number of units then you will probably not be aiming for the more individual look. You could vary the style slightly, however, if you made a conscious decision to design and equip some of the cottages to a higher standard than others. These would then merit a higher weekly rental and perhaps a higher star rating.

Taste

This is such an individual matter that it is impossible to generalise. You will not be scored on taste when you are being quality assured but it probably influences the assessors, albeit subconsciously. It is important to remember that whatever you think you are achieving in terms of design and decoration, a proportion of your guests will not like it. Victorian pine furniture will be thought of as just 'old', red walls are 'too bright' and that painstakingly restored flagstone floor will be classed as 'cold'. Stick to your guns – for every visitor who remarks on these aspects there will be far more who really appreciate what you have done to make the property 'different'.

Think of the sort of visitor you want to attract. You are attempting to provide an environment that they will like and appreciate. If it is a purely family market you want then furniture and furnishings should be practical, bright, inviting, and easily kept and cleaned. If you want to attract couples you could be more adventurous in colour and design and install more stylistic or individual furniture.

The rooms

These should be looked at from both a practical and a decorative standpoint, though which is the more important has to be decided by you. Where does the balance lie in the design? I think it depends on the room. In the kitchen practicality is the more important. In the sitting room you can tip the balance more towards the decorative.

Kitchens

The design of kitchens should always be practical. Ideally you need enough space to include all the expected equipment as well as leaving your guests room to move. There should be plenty of clear worktop and generous cupboard space, especially if the cottage sleeps six or more. The floor should be long-lasting and easy to keep clean – vinyl, vinyl tiles, ceramic or quarry tiling or possibly wood or laminate, though the last two can be damaged by water. If you are choosing vinyl, a dappled, marbled or patterned finish hides any small stains or marks.

The units themselves should be robust with adjustable hinges – they will get hard wear from some visitors. Whether you choose to install expensive kitchen units built to last or less expensive ones which can be replaced after a few years is a decision you will have to make. It is wise to choose a style and finish that is long lasting and does not date.

Pale coloured worktops will show up any damage done to them. You may think that you have countered any problem by equipping the kitchen with more than one chopping board but this is not always successful. Darker surfaces with a marbled or muted pattern will hide the occasional knife mark and look smart as well.

Even though the kitchen has to be a very practical room, try to create a sense of style, particularly if your visitors will be eating their meals there. Match or contrast the colours of the flooring and the units. Kitchen units come in all sorts of styles and colours and often it costs no more to buy interesting looking units than plainer ones.

Use kitchen and bathroom emulsion on the walls – it is easy to wipe clean – and, of course, tile the walls above the worktops. If your cooker is freestanding and separate from the units and does not have an upright panel at the back, protect the wall behind it with a pane of heat proof glass. It is cheap to buy, easy to keep clean and looks stylish.

Kitchen lighting should be bright with work surfaces and the cooker well lit. Individual spotlights are excellent for this. If your visitors are eating in the kitchen, can you install lighting that will permit them to cut down on the main lighting and use softer lighting over the table only? This will make for a much better atmosphere in the evenings.

Bathrooms

Installing white units means that you are not confined to any specific colour scheme when decorating the bathrooms. Steel baths (or cast iron) are best, but if you are fitting an acrylic bath make sure it is installed properly and does not creak when someone steps into it! The area round the bath should be tiled of course and if you have a shower over the bath this area needs to be tiled right up to the ceiling. Power showers are excellent, but even if you cannot install one of these there should be a good flow of water from the showerhead and not just a frustrating trickle.

A mirror over the hand basin with shaver socket and light is important. Do not put it too high up on the wall or the smaller guests will have difficulty seeing themselves in it!

Cheap seats for the WC are not worth buying. They are very flimsy and can be damaged too easily. More robust seats will have several rubber or plastic stops to make contact with the top rim – which will extend their life.

It is not always advisable to wallpaper bathrooms unless you are confident that the ventilation is good. Kitchen and bathroom emulsion is practical and long-lasting and you can change the colour of your bathroom at any time by repainting the walls. If you have a lot of wall space and feel that the bathroom looks a little bland then it is easy to brighten the room by putting up some decoration – not normal pictures as they will suffer with the steam – but plaster panels or decorative items of some sort perhaps. Fully tiled bathrooms look clean and modern, but the new wet wall material is becoming increasingly popular. It can be bought in a variety of colours and comes under several different trade names. It is the easiest of all walls to clean as there is no grouting and the finish is smooth. It is also ideal for shower areas, as the connecting seals make it totally waterproof. It is far from cheap but, once installed, it should never need replacing.

The flooring choices you have are ceramic tiling (very cold in northern climates) or vinyl (from a roll). There can be a problem with vinyl tiles as too much water splashed onto the floor can cause the tiles to rise at the edges, however well laid. Carpeting is not really an option. It is not at all hygienic in the bathroom and is very unpopular with guests from the USA for this reason.

Recessed ceiling lighting in bathrooms gives a very streamlined look and is practical in conjunction with the shaver lights over the mirror. Any light switches need to be of the cord pull type or should be sited outside the bathroom.

Bedrooms

These should always be welcoming. Blue is calming but can easily look cold on a dull day. Using yellow, for example, gives a sunny feel to the room whatever the weather. It is maybe not a good idea to decorate a bedroom exclusively in pink. It may be your favourite colour but is very off putting if the occupant is a teenage boy!

Try to strike a balance between the over decorative and the minimalist with some pictures on the walls, sufficiently full curtains that keep out the light, good lighting, good quality bed linen and not too many ornaments. As mentioned before, waiting for the sales to buy bed linen means that you can pick up real bargains at very reasonable prices. The colours of the less expensive bed linen often look washed out after a while and the fasteners on the cheaper duvet covers become damaged easily.

Ideally, the beds themselves should be of good quality with very good mattresses. As mentioned earlier, buy five-foot wide beds rather than doubles if you can. Fabric headboards may become a problem after a while, as well as being unhygienic – a wooden headboard can be cleaned more easily.

When wallpapering the bedrooms, keep an extra roll or two of the paper in case of emergencies. Wallpaper designs only seem to last a season nowadays and you may not be able to buy a matching roll later. Using a vinyl wallpaper means you can erase most marks and there are so many colours and designs available that you will be spoiled for choice.

Furniture in the bedrooms should follow a general theme or style. The quality assurance schemes are universally keen on matching furniture but this is not always practical or desirable. It can give a rather standardised look to the room, as though you had bought the whole set of furniture and furnishings as a package deal. If you are using different types of wood for the dressing table and bedside cabinets and they look good together, do not be put off. As long as the room has co-ordination and looks as if you intended it to be that way, rather than throwing together a lot of odd pieces of furniture, that is fine.

This is a room in which you do need soft carpeting. It will not get hard wear like the sitting room, so you can perhaps buy a better quality. A different way of looking at the situation is to buy cheaper carpeting but some very stylish rugs to go by the bedside.

Lighting in the bedrooms should be soft, though the lights by the bedside need to be bright enough to read by. The overall lighting in the room should be bright enough to allow the guests to see clearly inside the wardrobe and drawers.

Halls and stairways

You may get scuff marks on the walls with the passage of luggage or even pushchairs on occasion. Painted walls are the easiest option – keep some spare paint in the shed for emergency use. Emulsion dries quickly and you may have to repaint these areas more frequently than others as they often get hard usage. Having a dado rail with pine panelling underneath can protect the walls from some damage, but this is an area which inevitably over the letting year will get hard usage.

To prevent any accidents halls, landings and especially staircases should all be very well lit with no dark corners. Lights should be workable by two- or three-way switches, ensuring that no one has to walk far along the landing or corridor before reaching a switch. A varnished wooden stair with no carpeting can be dangerously slippery to guests who walk about in bare feet or socks.

Sitting rooms and dining rooms

This is where your visitors will spend most of their time so the emphasis should be on comfort. It should be warm, restful and inviting. There should be plenty of sofas and easy chairs with lots of cushions for extra support and decoration. Use colour to advantage in your sitting room. Warm colours such as terracotta, restful colours such as green and bright colours for the walls, such as yellow, all look good. If your room does not get much sun then you can counteract this with colour. Wallpaper or paint the room in pale gold, for example, and hang some attractive pictures on the walls. The curtains should be lined and generous in width and the carpets of good quality or possibly less expensive but with rugs. Choose a design with speckles or a slight pattern in it to disguise the occasional mark. Use pictures, mirrors and photographs to add personality to the room.

If you are a collector of paperbacks, put a small library in the room for the guests. You will probably find that they will bring their own books on holiday and having read them, will leave some behind to add to your collection. Once you have read a magazine, instead of throwing it out, put it in a cottage – as long as it is not too old. You do not want the place looking like a doctor's waiting room! A small video/DVD and CD library help to give a relaxed feel to the room and make your guest feel at home. Make sure the videos/DVDs are suitable for families, or you will have to remember to sift out some when children come to visit. Some cottage owners provide fresh flowers or perhaps a basket of fruit for their visitors, though this is difficult when the cottages are located far from any shops.

Other furniture you provide for the room should be attractive as well as functional – a dresser to hold games and tourist information, a sideboard with mirror, occasional tables and table lamps. Do not pack the room with furniture though or this will give too crowded a feel when all your visitors are sitting there.

If you have an open fire or stove this will be the focal point, especially in the colder months. In these days of central heating, many of your visitors will never have used a real fire before and they may have difficulty in lighting it and keeping it going. Make sure the fire is set ready for use when they arrive and offer assistance if they need it. The secret is to have a liberal supply of kindling or fire lighters. Some visitors, unfortunately, are too embarrassed to confess that they cannot get the fire going so you might find that they have given up in the end, unless you can help them.

Good central lighting in a room is the starting point. You might also think about using dimmer switches in the sitting room to give added ambience. The style and design of lighting available in the shops is very varied and you can create almost any mood you wish by choosing wisely. It should be possible to light the sitting room with just the table lamps to give a softer feel in the evenings. Wall lights are another option here, as is a standard lamp or up lighters.

For a dining area, lights suspended over the main table are very attractive and create a mood for dining. Those that have an adjustable height are excellent. European visitors are accustomed to sitting long over their meals, particularly in the evenings. The dining chairs should be comfortable and the table of a generous enough size to easily seat the advertised number of people, with space for occasional guests if possible.

Check points

Some of the main points concerning the design and decorating of your cottages are:

◆ There is a vast choice in overall style for your properties. You can be just as successful in creating a very clean, simple look with some special feature as going for one of the more decorative schemes.

◆ Taste is so individual that it is hard to please everyone. However, you must consider your market and try to design and decorate your cottages to satisfy as broad a range of criteria as possible.

◆ Kitchens should be practical. Good lighting, sufficient units in a style which will not date and easily cleaned flooring are all important. There should be enough space for cupboard and refrigerator doors to be able to open wide when necessary.

◆ Bathrooms should also be practical. Good quality baths are important as are sufficiently powerful showers. There should be lighting over the mirror above the wash basin in addition to the main light. Floors must be able to withstand a certain amount of water.

- Bedrooms can be more decorative. Use welcoming colours for your visitors. Furniture need not match exactly, but try to achieve an overall cohesive feel to the room. Bedside lights should be bright enough to read by and a dimmer switch is a nice touch for the main light.

- Beds should be comfortable with very good mattresses. These need to be protected with mattress covers. Buy king sized beds rather than doubles.

- Halls and stairways get hard usage. If you use emulsion on the walls it is quick and easy to touch up any marked areas, even between visits. Hall(s) and stairways need very good lighting for safety reasons.

- The emphasis is on comfort in the sitting room, with easy chairs and sofas with cushions. Counteract any lack of sun with warm or bright colours.

- A fire or stove will prove a focal point for the sitting room though some visitors will be unused to one and may need help with lighting it.

- Include a small library of books, and a collection of CDs and videos/DVDs if possible, to give a relaxed feel to the the room.

- A light suspended over the main table gives a lovely ambience for dining in the evenings.

PROGRESS PLAN

While thinking about decorating and designing your cottage or cottages:

1. Will you be choosing a particular style of decoration for the properties or will it be fairly plain? Note down any special colours or designs you want to try out.

----

2. What particular features of colour, décor and design do you like in a bedroom? Can you translate these for use in the bedrooms of the cottages, without making them all the same?

----

3. How do you plan to make the sitting/dining room areas of the cottages comfortable and relaxing? What will you include in the way of extras?

----

4. Draw up a complete list of all the main items of furniture you will have to buy for all the cottages. Prioritise the list so that the essentials are at the beginning and those items that are 'nice to have' are at the end. In round figures, calculate what this will cost.

In conclusion

Design and decoration are usually a very personal choice. But whether you adapt a well known style for use or simply decide to create your own style, working from the colours you like, the result must be pleasing to the majority of the guests. Decorate the properties with your main market in mind. It is wise not to follow fashion trends too closely as they will have a short 'shelf life' and the cottages will look dated after a while.

Now that you have a clearer idea of how the properties will look and the amount of furniture and furnishings you need to buy, let's move on to the important area of finance.

9

Sorting Out the Finance

You are confident now that your plan can succeed. You know the kind of property you are looking for and where to find it. You have thought through the design and décor of your new property or properties and you are ready to move on.

It is time to consider the financial side of the plan. How are you going to afford the new business? Will you have enough cash in hand from your previous house to act as a healthy percentage deposit for the purchase of the new property and any building work or alterations? Estimating the cost of the building work in advance is always difficult and you may find it more expensive than you planned for. You will also have living costs while setting up the business – it takes a while for a business to become profitable.

You will possibly need to raise extra finance by way of mortgage, loan or grant, so will have to draw up a business plan. It need not be complicated but in order to cover the necessary ground, it should be thorough.

The business plan

A good business plan will focus your mind as well as help you to get some financial support. You need to include all the information to convince your bank, building society or grant body that your business will be viable and that you are sufficiently knowledgeable about the new venture to make it a success.

What sort of information do you include?

1 Your business and the service

Ask yourself these questions about the background to your idea:

◆ What exactly is your idea or plan?

◆ How long have you been planning this new self catering business?

◆ How much do you know about self catering or the tourist industry?

◆ Have you carried out any work so far on the new business? If so, what is the extent of this?

◆ Have you had any direct experience of self catering?

◆ Who are to be the owners of the business? You and your partner? Your family? Are friends or business partners involved?

Think about what service you will provide. You need to know:

◆ Exactly what your service is to be: small cottage, large chalet park, conversion of a building, etc. Explain the kind of self catering you intend to provide.

- How and why it will be different from any other holiday accommodation in the area.

- Why people will choose to come to you rather than go to other self catering establishments and what will make your facilities more attractive to prospective guests.

- How you see the future and plans for improvement or expansion once you are set up. Perhaps you will move into other areas such as running workshops or training courses.

- How you see yourself earning enough to tide you over in the off season months.

- Any weaknesses or problem areas you can foresee. It helps here to show you have thought things through properly.

2 Your market and competitors

Who is your market? You need to know:

- What sort of visitors you are aiming at. Do not limit yourself to only one field. It will make a big difference to the facilities you are planning to provide. Why are you planning to attract those visitors? What are you going to do to make your property attractive to them? You could be planning downstairs bedrooms for those who have difficulty with stairs or you could be aiming for a 'green' award from the tourist board. You could be making your properties all very individual for the more discerning visitor. Perhaps you are installing open fires or stoves for walkers and climbers and those who come in the winter months.

- How big this market is. Can you prove, with statistics, that this market sector is increasing? For example, if you are planning to attract outdoor enthusiasts, you might show that more people than ever are taking this sort of holiday. Find figures for your area. Your National Tourist Board should have the statistics for visitor trends in previous years on their industry websites. Can you increase the range of your market by offering special interest holidays? You might offer discounts for groups and families booking more than one property at a time.

♦ If you have already started the business in a small way, to mention the numbers of visitors you have had and any trends you see developing. Work out what sort of return you have. Is the level of bookings you have already reached looking promising?

You need to know who your competitors are:

♦ If there are several self catering properties in your chosen area, show you have done your homework, that you know your competitors and any benefits or disadvantages that their businesses display.

♦ Why will people come to you rather than to them? Show you have done your market research properly. You must know how to compete successfully with the opposition, otherwise your business will not be viable.

3 Marketing your business

You need to know:

♦ How your holiday properties will meet the visitors' specific needs. Work out how your prices compare with others in the business; how you can provide that extra special experience for your guests.

♦ How you will advertise your properties. You might use your own website or your own brochure, commercial websites, magazines, newspapers, agencies or the Tourist Board. Are there deadlines for any of this advertising and, if so, can you still meet them for the coming season?

♦ How you are planning for repeat business. If you are making a particular effort to attract visitors back again what percentage of repeat business are you aiming for?

♦ Whether you have any visitors interested already. Self catering holidays are often booked months ahead, with deposits sent at the time of booking. What bookings do you have already and how much have you made from them?

♦ Whether you want to plan any associated business, for example craft workshops.

◆ How you will find potential visitors of the kind you want. How will you target the right customers?

◆ When you are hoping to start your business, if you have not already.

4 The management

Things to ask yourself about those in charge:

◆ Who are to be the managers of your business? What style of management will there be – 'hands on' or employing others?

◆ What are their particular strengths and how will they overcome any weaknesses? Perhaps only one of them is really confident on the computer but the other is better at talking to the guests. Or one of them is really organised when it comes to recording the bookings and payments while the other is excellent at designing the brochures and does all the housekeeping.

◆ Can you provide useful and relevant background information on the managers? Have they had any previous experience in the same sort of business or at least something similar? Is anyone experienced in web design or accounting?

◆ Are there any business supporters – mentors – to provide informal assistance?

◆ Just how enthusiastic and committed are they?

◆ How much time and money will they (all) contribute?

◆ Is any training needed? If so, in which fields?

And about the staff:

◆ Will extra staff be needed? Will they be full-time, part-time or seasonal?

◆ Will staff need any training? If so, in what exactly?

◆ Is the management aware of the legal responsibilities when employing full or part-time staff?

5 *Financial forecasts*

◆ Work out a realistic income and expenditure forecast for the next three years, breaking down the figures into months.

◆ Produce a cash flow forecast showing how much money you expect to be moving in and out of your bank account(s) and when. Show you have considered all the key factors, such as seasonal variations or staff wages. At what time will the business be cash positive – more cash coming in than going out?

◆ For your forecast, list all the assumptions you have made – weekly prices, timing of deposits and balance payments, etc. Small business advisors at banks, Business Link and Enterprise Agencies will help you put your forecasts together free of charge.

◆ Is there a maximum annual income you can expect from the properties? If so, what is it? What kind of percentage of this do you expect in the first three years as you build up the business – perhaps 35%, 55% and 70%?

◆ What will your charges be for any extra activities you are planning such as craft workshops or training courses?

6 *Financial requirements*

◆ The cash flow forecast will show how much finance you will need. Do you also need contingency funding? State how much you will need, when you want it and in what form. You might ask for an overdraft facility and a loan from a bank, for example.

◆ What will the money be used for? It might be for building work, furniture and carpets, a computer, printing a brochure or perhaps the design of a new website.

◆ Give proof that you can afford it. Looking at your cash flow forecast, does it allow for repayments on the loan?

◆ Work out any costs involved in recruiting and training staff or perhaps in management training.

◆ What sort of support do you already have? Give details of architects, surveyors, accountants, solicitors, etc.

7 *Appendices*

This should be supporting information for the main document and should include:

- Any cash flow tables, income figures, weekly price lists for the properties, etc.

- Market research data you have referred to in the document, such as Tourist Board statistics for your area and for self catering in general.

- Any technical specifications such as tenders for building work, surveyors' reports, costings for furniture and fittings, etc.

- Planning permission for a new build or conversion if appropriate – include any plans.

8 *The summary*

Although this is a summary of your whole plan, *it goes at the beginning*. Remember that some reviewers may only read this overall summary, so use it to make your key points – they can always check the additional detail in the body of the main report. It will be read by people not familiar with your business so avoid technical jargon and use it to summarise six main areas:

1 Your self catering properties and their main advantages.
2 The opportunities in the tourism business.
3 The management.
4 Your record to date (if any).
5 Financial projections.
6 Funding requirements.

9 *Presenting your document*

- Keep it short, focusing only on what the reader needs to know. Many business plans are too long.

- Make it look professional. Give it a title page and put on a cover if possible. Include a list of contents.

- Re-read it yourself and get a friend to read it. Does it really give a good picture of your business? Is it realistic?

- Do you know any expert advisors you could ask to check it? Time spent now, before presenting it officially, is time well spent for your future.

Cash flow

It is very difficult indeed to estimate income and expenditure before your business has even started. You may not need to produce a cash flow forecast – especially if you do not need that extra finance and will not be producing a business plan. However, it is well worth making the effort. We had to draw one up when we were applying for some financial help and we're glad we did! It certainly focuses the mind as it is only when you get down to that fine detail of expected income and probable expenditure that reality bites! It changed our minds on some of the wilder items of expenditure and made us find ways of supplementing the basic income we expected, particularly in the early years when it took time to build up the business and we were slowly becoming known.

It need not be all that complicated. We drew up a five-page cash flow forecast for five financial years. Each page had a column for each month and a column at the start for the income sources and the items of expenditure (see Figure 1). Excel is a very good tool for this but an ordinary table in Word is perfectly sufficient. The income is broken down by 'source'. Here we had direct letting income from the holiday properties and then, when we realised that this was not going to be sufficient, we had to find income from other sources. We made plans to start running workshops for crafts and possibly training courses in part of the building, mainly in the quieter months.

We listed the expenditure under headings of insurance, heating and lighting, telephone and computer, car and travel, postage and stationery, printing, advertising, business rates, bank charges and loan and/or mortgage repayments. At this stage it was difficult to estimate costs but we tried to base it on other similar properties and figures from websites and printing companies.

Cash flow forecast for year to March 2006	April	May	June	July	Etc.
Income					
Self catering	200	550	750	950	
Workshops	350	150	200	200	
Training	0	0	0	0	
Total income	**550**	**700**	**950**	**1150**	
Expenditure					
Insurance	55	55	55	55	
Heating and lighting	90	85	80	80	
Telephone and computer	45	50	50	45	
Car and travel	88	90	110	80	
Postage and stationery	25	20	20	20	
Printing	200	0	0	0	
Advertising	450	300	100	100	
Business rates	0	500	0	0	
Mortgage/loan repayments	450	450	450	450	
Bank charges	15	15	15	15	
Furniture	2000	900	0	0	
Contents	500	100	50	20	
Capital items	2500	0	0	0	
Total expenditure	**6418**	**2565**	**930**	**865**	
Opening balance	0	−5868	−7733	−7713	−7428
Monthly movement	−5868	−1865	+20	+285	
Closing balance	−5868	−7733	−7713	−7428	

Fig. 1. Sample cash flow forecast.

A major item was capital expenditure, particularly at the start-up of the business, and of course the purchase of all the furniture, carpets and small items needed for the properties before we could begin letting. The list grew depressingly long but it pays to be honest with yourself.

◆ **TOP TIP** ◆

Figures plucked from the air or a vague approach can only lead to disaster when you realise you haven't asked for sufficient financial aid at the beginning of your venture.

Your opening balance for the first month of the financial year is £0. Add the difference between the total income and the total expenditure for the month – it will probably be negative – and you have the monthly movement. The closing balance is the sum of the opening balance and the monthly movement (a negative figure in Figure 1).

That closing balance is carried forward to be the opening balance for the next month. The whole process is repeated for each month in turn. As you increase your earnings while keeping expenditure at a reasonable level, month after month, the balance should eventually become positive.

Perhaps you can see the obvious problem. To set up your properties you will need to buy furniture and contents. You will need to advertise well in advance of the opening date so you will need a web page and brochures. You may be joining the Tourist Board – paying for membership, quality assurance and advertising. All this happens before you even get your first deposit, let alone welcome your first visitor, but it is all very necessary. It means that for the first period of time, you will not have a positive balance, let alone enough to live on.

This is where your savings come in. It is essential to have some money in reserve from the purchase of your previous property. You will need it to carry you through the difficult first few months.

You will also be able to see from your figures the level of finance you will require from outside sources. The whole process will definitely concentrate your mind on your earning power!

Grants

As we have established, if you are intending to build new holiday properties or to convert an older building, the costs will be high. There will also be the costs of new equipment, furniture and furnishings, both for your own office and the cottages. You may however qualify for a grant. You have to decide whether your start-up is likely to be eligible for one and whether such a grant is worth applying for.

Do not waste time trying to get a grant unless you are prepared to jump over certain hurdles first.

◆ You must be prepared to put up some of your own money. It is very rare for a grant to finance 100% of the costs of any project. The percentage is more likely to be in the region of 15 to 20%.

◆ Grants are only available for specific projects.

◆ You must have a business plan. If you are applying for funds for a specific area of costs, then you will have to alter the business plan to emphasise that area.

◆ Grant schemes always impose some restrictions and you must abide by these. The project cannot already be underway and must in some way reflect the aims of the grant provider. You need to be able to demonstrate that your project will not take place at all or at least will not succeed as well without the grant.

So what grants are available?

◆ The location you are choosing to set up your self catering business may entitle you to a grant, for instance if it is in an economically depressed area with high unemployment, as some rural regions are.

◆ Because you are choosing to move into tourism, you may be at an advantage because it is one of the areas that grant funding has specifically targeted.

◆ Training activities are looked on favourably by grant bodies. If you or any staff you might employ require training in some relevant field there would almost certainly be grants available.

- Some grants are intended to help new businesses and to boost employment in the area. Can you show that you will be employing a number of staff, albeit on a seasonal basis? They may also consider you to be employed through this new business.

Who should you contact?

The first stop should be your local Business Link or Enterprise Agency. These business support organisations will provide you with a list of grant schemes. You may also be able to speak to a business advisor who will help you narrow down the range of available schemes to those that you should approach.

When you come to submitting a proposal, it will involve filling in a form or a series of forms. You need to explain your self catering project and exactly what you need the money for, in the best possible light. You will also have to give a detailed description and an explanation of the benefits the project will have, with reference to the particular aims of the grant body.

Do not expect an immediate answer. Grants by local councils, for example, usually take up to six weeks to process. National or European grants take considerably longer – a waiting time of up to six months is possible.

If you are awarded the grant after all your hard work, the payments are usually made in instalments at fixed periods of time. You will need to keep detailed records of how you spend the money – the grant bodies will want to monitor this.

Check points

There is a great deal of financial information to digest in this chapter. The major points to note are:

- If you are going to need some sort of finance for the set up of your self catering business then you should draw up a business plan. The summary of the whole plan goes at the beginning of the document followed by the information you need to include:

– your business and the service it will provide;

– your market and competitors;

– marketing your business;

– the management;

– financial forecasts;

– financial requirements.

There should also be appendices with supporting statistics and financial data.

♦ Drawing up a cash flow table before your business starts is essential, both for inclusion in any business plan and also for a reality check for you. It should include all items of income and expenditure you are likely to have.

♦ There are often grants available for the initial set up of your business. If you are prepared to carry out all the research and administration necessary, approach your local Enterprise Agency or Business Link for information on grant schemes you might be eligible for.

PROGRESS PLAN

Have you considered all the financial implications of your business venture? Under the following main headings of the business plan, note down your initial thoughts with regard to your planned project.

1. How will you present your project in the business plan? Sketch out some of the background and explain what sort of service you will provide.

----

2. Explain the visitor market(s) you are aiming for and what you will be doing specifically to attract that market. Have you any evidence that this is the right market for your area?

----

3. Have you thought about how you will be marketing your business? Where will you advertise?

----

4. What strengths do you and your partner and/or family have to bring to the business? Do you feel that you and/or your partner will need any training or updating of your skills?

----

5. You should be working out some ballpark figures for costs at this stage. How much will you have available to invest in your new business in total? What are the main costs involved in your plan? These could include buying an already functioning business, buying a property to convert or building. If you are intending to build extra cottages, cost these in as well. If you are buying furniture and furnishings, cost these in too.

----

6. Do your figures add up or will you need extra finance? Where will you apply for this finance? Are you also hoping to receive a grant? Which grant body or bodies will you apply to?

Moving on

You have now carried out some of the basic groundwork as far as the finance is concerned. You know how to draw up a business plan and, as part of that, you can create a cash flow table which will give you a very good idea of how you stand financially with your self catering plan.

It can be a shock when the plans start to turn into reality and you discover exactly how much money you actually have and how much finance you will need to achieve your aim. It is necessary, however, to go through the process so that you can look at the project realistically.

Make any adjustments necessary to your dreams, to be more in line with financial reality – then check that your total business plan will still provide you with a viable income overall.

10

The National Tourist Boards

England, Scotland, Wales and Northern Ireland all have their own Tourist Boards, each with an official website. Each Tourist Board also has a website for the tourism industry itself which you will find very useful. This will give you tourism statistics, business advice and contact details for agencies which will help you start up and run your business. It is worthwhile spending some time looking at the relevant industry website to check its scope and contacts.

England

VisitBritain markets Britain to the rest of the world and England to the British. Their publicised mission is to build the value of tourism by creating world class destination brands and marketing campaigns. VisitBritain also builds partnerships with – and provides insights to – other organisations which have a stake in British and English tourism.

In addition to its responsibilities for marketing England to the British, VisitBritain works in partnership with the National Tourist Boards in Northern Ireland, Scotland and Wales to promote an attractive image of Britain. It provides impartial tourism information and gathers essential market intelligence and insights for the UK tourism industry.

VisitBritain is funded by the Department for Culture, Media and Sport to promote Britain overseas as a tourism destination, and to lead and co-ordinate the domestic marketing of England.

- The official website for the tourist board is www.visitbritain.com

- The industry website is www.tourismtrade.org.uk

- See the Appendix for telephone numbers and other contact details for tourism in England.

Wales

The Wales Tourist Board is an Assembly Sponsored Public Body, answerable to the Minister for Economic Development of the Welsh Assembly Government. The Board was set up under the Development of Tourism Act 1969. Its publicised role is to support the tourism industry and to provide a strategic framework within which private enterprise can achieve sustainable growth and success, so improving the social and economic well being of Wales.

- The official website for the tourist board is www.visitwales.com. The website provides all its information in Welsh and English.

- The industry website is www.wtbonline.gov.uk

- See the Appendix for telephone numbers and other contact details for tourism in Wales.

Scotland

VisitScotland is the official tourist board for Scotland. Its publicity emphasises that it has a strategic role as the public sector agency providing leadership and direction for the development of Scottish tourism to get the maximum economic benefit for Scotland.

It exists to support the development of the tourism industry in Scotland and to market the country as a quality destination.

◆ Official website of the tourist board is www.visitscotland.com

◆ Website for the industry is www.scotexchange.net.

◆ See the Appendix for telephone numbers and other contact details for tourism in Scotland.

Northern Ireland

The Northern Ireland Tourist Board (NITB) is a non-departmental public body of the Department of Enterprise, Trade and Investment Northern Ireland, constituted under the Tourism (Northern Ireland) Order 1992. It is the body responsible for the development, promotion and marketing of Northern Ireland as a tourist destination.

◆ The Official Northern Ireland Tourist Board website is www.discovernorthernireland.com

◆ The industry website is www.nitb.com

◆ See the Appendix for telephone numbers and other contact details for tourism in Northern Ireland.

Under the Tourism (Northern Ireland) Order 1992, everyone who provides any form of tourist accommodation in Northern Ireland must possess a valid certificate for the premises, issued by the Northern Ireland Tourist Board. This applies to hotels, guesthouses, B&B establishments, self catering accommodation and hostels. Anyone who provides or offers accommodation to tourists without being in possession of the certificate is guilty of an offence and, on conviction, becomes liable to a fine of up to £2,500 or imprisonment.

Quality Assurance

All the Tourist Boards run Quality Assurance schemes for self catering accommodation. In signing up to these, your properties will be inspected by a Quality Assurance Assessor who will give them a grade (or star rating) according to the various criteria in force in the different parts of Britain.

At present England, Wales and Scotland are working towards a set of common standards for Quality Assurance for self catering properties, which will apply throughout.

Northern Ireland has its own distinct scheme.

You are advised to contact your own particular Tourist Board for the set of standards on Quality Assurance that will apply to your self catering establishment. You should do this when you are setting up and every year after that, if you wish to be assessed.

The common standards

There will be eight main areas where quality grading will take place:

Exterior

This involves three main sections:

◆ appearance of the buildings themselves;

◆ grounds, gardens and parking areas;

◆ environment and setting.

Cleanliness

In view of its perceived importance, cleanliness is assessed as a separate aspect. It is looked at in the four main areas of the property:

◆ corridors, hallways, stairways, dining room, sitting room;

◆ bedrooms;

◆ bathrooms;

◆ kitchen.

Management efficiency

This judges how you respond to the guests and how well you run the establishment:

◆ pre-arrival procedures including your website;

◆ welcome and arrival procedure;

◆ guest information in the separate units, including any personal touches.

Public areas – dining room, sitting room, hallways, stairs, corridors

These are assessed in different components:

◆ decoration;

◆ flooring;

◆ furniture, furnishings and fittings;

◆ lighting and heating;

◆ space, comfort and ease of use.

Bedrooms

These are assessed on the same components as for the sitting room, etc, but with some additions:

◆ decoration;

◆ flooring;

◆ furniture, furnishings and fittings;

◆ lighting and heating;

◆ beds;

◆ bedding and bedlinen;

◆ space, comfort and ease of use.

Bathrooms and WCs

Bathrooms have their own particular criteria in assessing a cottage for a Quality Assurance Standard:

◆ decoration;

◆ flooring;

◆ fixtures, fittings, sanitary ware;

◆ lighting, heating and ventilation;

◆ space, comfort and ease of use.

Kitchen

Of the very greatest importance in any self catering property, the kitchen is assessed on:

◆ decoration;

◆ flooring;

◆ fittings and furniture;

◆ lighting, heating and ventilation;

◆ electrical equipment;

◆ crockery, cutlery and glassware;

◆ kitchen ware, pans and utensils;

◆ space, comfort and ease of use.

Additional facilities

This is, of course, only applicable to some self catering businesses:

◆ laundry;

◆ recreation;

◆ reception, bar, shop, restaurant.

There are also certain minimum entry requirements for the whole scheme, which will result in the one star rating. In order to achieve a higher rating, it is also necessary to meet the level of quality and condition specified in the different quality indicators. There are specific additional requirements to obtain a particular grade. The areas assessed for these minimum requirements include:

◆ general requirements;

◆ maintenance;

◆ health, safety and security;

◆ exterior;

◆ cleanliness;

◆ management efficiency;

◆ public areas;

◆ kitchens;

◆ bedrooms;

◆ bathrooms.

Local variations

England

Self catering establishments in England are encouraged to participate in the National Quality Assurance Standards (NQAS). Participation offers a number of benefits such as:

◆ promotional opportunities at home and overseas, with a free independent listing on the VisitBritain and TravelEngland sites;

◆ detailed assessment debrief and report;

◆ Quality Assured ratings;

◆ free business information leaflets;

◆ free copy of English Tourism Council (formerly the English Tourist Board) newsletter for its Quality Assurance Standards.

You will need the detailed set of criteria for Quality Assurance when you are setting up your property – it can be downloaded from the website for the trade, www.tourismtrade.org.uk or you can get a hard copy by contacting VisitBritain.

Wales

Wales is in the process of assimilating the research recently carried out to obtain the tourist industry's viewpoint on the proposed amendments to the present Quality Assurance Scheme, considered necessary to achieve the overall common standard.

The detailed list of criteria in place for quality assurance can be obtained from the Wales Tourist Board (see the Appendix for address) or the industry website www.wtbonline.gov.uk

Participation in the scheme has the benefits of:

◆ access to the WTB website;

◆ the opportunity to take entries in the national and local guide books that promote inspected properties only;

◆ verbal feedback on the quality of the property followed by a full written report;

◆ having artwork and stickers to promote your star rating on your own business literature;

◆ being able to provide the visitor with an indication of quality when they are making their booking.

Scotland

Scotland's Quality Assurance system was devised in 1996 after extensive consultation and market research with visitors and the trade. It is a development of an earlier system introduced in 1985. It is now in the process of incorporating the common standards into this scheme.

The benefits of joining the scheme are publicised by VisitScotland as follows:

◆ not only will your Quality Advisor assess your property on an annual basis but they can give a wide range of advice on a one-to-one basis relating to the tourism network and all the opportunities and information available;

◆ advertising in *Where to Stay* accommodation guides;

◆ advertising in the full range of VisitScotland brochures including Ski Scotland, Winter Activities, Autumn Gold, etc;

◆ reassuring visitors of the quality standard of your accommodation;

◆ having leaflets displayed and distributed at UK and overseas exhibitions;

◆ being featured on the website www.visitscotland.com.

The Quality Assurance Scheme runs from August each year to July the next and your self catering property could be visited by an assessor any time over this period. Advisory visits are available to new and existing members of the Scheme (for a fee). The advisor will visit your property and give you an accurate reflection of current standards and also specific advice on how to improve.

Although there is no membership fee, if businesses want to participate in marketing opportunities offered by VisitScotland and the 'hubs', they will have to be Quality Assured. For example, participation in the QA scheme is a condition of appearing on the website visitscotland.com.

For details of the scheme, see the website www.scotexchange.net or contact the Scottish Tourist Board, Visitscotland (contact details in the Appendix).

Northern Ireland
The Northern Ireland Tourist Board regulates all visitor accommodation and requires a wide range of criteria to be met. You will have to obtain various documents, including authorisation from

your divisional planning service (where applicable), the fire authority and the environmental health department of your district council. Each of these bodies will give you information about the requirements.

A Board advisor will conduct an inspection to determine if the premises are suitable to be allocated to the self-catering category. You will be charged a fee for every unit you intend to let, subject to a maximum of £250.

Once your certificate is awarded, your establishment will be inspected every year to ensure that the requirements continue to be met.

The system has five star classifications and divides into objective and subjective elements. The classification is judged by the objective elements – the presence or absence of certain facilities. However, if the facilities are not of sufficient quality, the premises may not be classified at all.

As well as the checklist of facilities other elements are taken into account.

- Code of conduct:
  - High standards of courtesy, cleanliness and service.
  - Accurate description of the facilities and the property in all literature and by word of mouth.
  - Clear information on prices, charges or extras, etc.
  - Adherence to stated prices.
  - Dealing promptly and courteously with enquiries, bookings, payments, etc.
  - Allowing a NI Tourist Board representative access to the establishment on request.

- General requirements
  - To have the necessary clearance by the relevant authorities (see before).
  - All fixtures, fittings, etc to be clean and in a sound condition.
  - All promotional literature to be accurate.

- Prices to include VAT (if applicable).
- All units cleaned and checked between guests.
- Visitors must be provided with a key to the entrance of their cottage (and to the building if applicable).
- If the owner lives off site, name, address and phone number must be displayed together with those of the emergency services.
- Gardens and outside areas must be well maintained.
- Basic clothes drying and ironing equipment must be provided.

◆ Information for guests. Full details of the sleeping accommodation must be provided in advance and in addition, information on:
  - Car parking near the cottage.
  - Arrangements for pets.
  - Distance of unit from shop, post office, etc.
  - Distance from nearest public transport.
  - Whether or not arrangements can be made for advance ordering of groceries, etc.
  - Nature of water supply.
  - Type of energy supply.
  - Electricity voltage if not standard.
  - Suitability for children.
  - Information on activities in the area.
  - Map and/or directions to the property.
  - Price list with 'extras'.

A complete inventory of the facilities provided by the premises is made and these are assessed for quality. There are additional measures of quality for particular star gradings.

At present (2005) the Quality Assurance Scheme in Northern Ireland is under review. The new scheme to be created as a result of that review will require legislation before it can be implemented. There is no date set as yet for this implemetation.

You are advised to contact the Northern Ireland Tourist Board (contact details in the Appendix) for details of the scheme or see their industry website www.nitb.com.

Check points

+ The National Tourist Boards are:
    – Visitbritain in England, website www.visitbritain.com
    – Wales Tourist Board, website www.visitwales.com
    – Visitscotland in Scotland, website www.visitscotland.com
    – Northern Ireland Tourist Board, website
      www.discovernorthernireland.com

+ England, Scotland and Wales are moving towards a set of Common
  Standards on Quality Assurance while Northern Ireland has its own
  distinct scheme. The areas assessed under the Common Standards are:
    – exterior;
    – cleanliness;
    – management efficiency;
    – living room, dining room, halls, stairs;
    – bedrooms;
    – bathrooms;
    – kitchen;
    – additional facilities.

+ There are also certain minimum entry requirements for the whole
  scheme. These will apply to the one star rating and above. In order to
  achieve a higher rating, it is necessary to meet the level of quality and
  condition specified in the different quality indicators. There are also
  specific additional requirements to obtain a particular grade. These
  minimum requirements are set in the following areas:
    – general requirements including statutory obligations;
    – maintenance;
    – health, safety and security;
    – the exterior;
    – cleanliness;
    – management efficiency;
    – the rooms themselves.

+ Membership of the Quality Assurance Schemes has certain benefits
  emphasised by the Tourist Boards. These include:

- promotional opportunities;
- access to advertising on the website and in brochures;
- reassurance of visitors;
- detailed feedback after the inspection.

◆ In Northern Ireland it is a statutory requirement that all holiday accommodation should be registered with the Tourist Board. The Quality Assurance Scheme divides into a checklist of facilities (also graded on quality) and the more subjective elements such as:
- a code of conduct;
- general requirements;
- information provided for guests.

PROGRESS PLAN

1. Select the Tourist Board relevant to you and check the website for information on Quality Assurance. Download the document(s) or send for a written copy.

_____
_____

2. Looking at the grading schemes, what star rating(s) will you be hoping to achieve? Make a list of any changes or improvements you will have to make to the cottage(s) to bring them up to this standard.

_____
_____

3. Looking at your list of changes or improvements, prioritise these based on the overall cost and the likelihood of you being in a position (financially, work involved, etc.) to respond to these in the next two months. If not – when could you carry out some of your larger priority items?

_____
_____

In conclusion

Depending on what part of Britain your business is in, the Tourist Board has a set of standards for Quality Assurance for the property. Most holiday cottage owners join a Quality Assurance Scheme for the benefits it bestows. It is sensible to look at the requirements of these schemes quite early on, so that you know to which standard you will be aspiring.

It is not necessary to keep trying to reach a higher standard. If you have a three star property, for example, with a total percentage which places you high in that band, then you might be perfectly content with this. You will find that you have a large number of guests who are very happy holidaying in your property. Why spend a lot of time and money trying to move into the four star grade if it is not necessary?

On the other hand, if you are ambitious to have four or even five star properties, go for it!

11

Other Quality Assurance Schemes

The National Tourist Boards run other important initiatives in addition to the main Quality Assurance Schemes. At the moment these are in connection with the environment, disability, and walkers and cyclists. It could be of considerable advantage to you to be assessed for a grading in one or other of these additional schemes, and to advertise as such, as this could bring in new visitors interested in staying in holiday cottages with these particular features.

Green Schemes

There is an increasing emphasis on a greener Britain. All the Tourist Boards have their schemes where you can work towards levels of compliance with a set of standards. In many cases there are grants available from agencies to help you to make your business more environmentally friendly.

Some of the actions you can take are as follows.

- Save water:
  - install spray tap applicators to reduce water flow;
  - install hippo bags in the cisterns;
  - buy water efficient A or B rated white goods;
  - collect rain water to use on the garden;
  - install dual flush toilet cisterns;
  - install showers rather than baths;
  - check and maintain taps to avoid dripping;
  - install self closing taps.

- Save energy:
  - buy white goods which display a high energy saving level;
  - insulate your properties well;
  - buy low energy light bulbs;
  - install solar panels;
  - install a wind turbine (which will probably require planning permission) or other form of renewable energy;
  - install thermostatic radiator valves;
  - check that entrance doors are well sealed;
  - use a high efficiency boiler (85% or over).

- Reduce, re-use and recycle waste:
  - re-use materials whenever possible;
  - tell visitors about recycling facilities in the area or provide them yourself;
  - buy in bulk to reduce packaging waste;
  - copy and print your literature on both sides of the paper.

- Take care with hazardous substances:
  - recycle toner and print cartridges;
  - do not use chemicals in the garden;
  - make sure the oil supply is safe;
  - use environmentally friendly detergents in the properties;

   – avoid solvent based paints, solvent chemicals. Use re-chargeable batteries.

- Use greener transport:
  – encourage visitors to use public transport;
  – promote walkers and cyclists by providing a lift from the station;
  – promote local walking and cycling routes with maps;
  – provide information on local bike hire;
  – provide information on excursions by public transport and local bus timetables;
  – offer cycle hire to visitors.

- Plan and build sympathetically with the environment:
  – review materials used for building;
  – insulate your properties well;
  – use local building materials from a sustainable source;
  – build energy and water efficient features into any new building or conversion;
  – use sustainable timber for your properties;
  – comply with legislation.

England

The Tourist Board in England has no green award scheme as such in place at the moment but it does run a one-day training event called Green Advantage for those in the tourism and leisure industries. It is aimed to improve environmental awareness and is publicised as offering significant business benefits to employees, managers and owners of organisations in the tourism industry. The course content is designed to help develop the skills, knowledge and understanding of green issues and actions for those who take part. At the end of the course each participant will receive a certificate and can obtain a free copy of the new Green Audit Kit, published by the English Tourism Council and the Countryside Agency, to assist with the implementation of their own environmental improvements.

You can obtain information on Green Advantage from the website for the tourism industry www.tourismtrade.org.uk.

Wales

The Tourist Board in Wales is committed to encouraging as many businesses as possible to work towards a sustainable approach to the environment in their day-to-day operations. They have issued a toolkit which lays out the principles of 'greener' tourism and helps businesses work towards the Green Dragon Standard. This consists of five stages – the first two being the most relevant to tourism small and medium sized companies. Companies achieving the standard receive a certificate and are featured on the Green Dragon website. Companies achieving level two or above are entitled to display the logo on stationery and marketing information. For information on the scheme you are advised to contact ARENA Network (see Appendix) which can also offer a European grant to small businesses to assist them to invest in measures for a cleaner environment.

Scotland

The Scottish Tourist Board runs the Green Tourism Business Scheme. The GTBS was established by VisitScotland in 1998, fully supported by Scottish Enterprise and Highlands and Islands Enterprise and with the technical assistance of SEA Ltd. It is an accredited VisitScotland Quality Assurance Scheme and is operated in Scotland by Green Business UK Ltd, a not-for-profit company, on behalf of VisitScotland. There are three levels of the GTBS you can achieve – the Bronze, Silver and Gold.

In order to gain any award you must be able to satisfactorily complete the measures in the compulsory section and you must implement a minimum number of measures in each technical section – management, communication, energy, water, purchasing, waste, transport and wildlife. The wildlife section is optional except for holiday parks. For full details of the scheme you should contact the Green Business Tourism Scheme – contact details in the Appendix.

Northern Ireland

Three tourism partnerships have joined forces to promote best environmental practice and sustainable tourism across their areas.

Causeway Coast and Glens Heritage Trust, Mourne Heritage Trust and South Armagh Tourism Initiative, assisted by the Northern Ireland Tourist board, are helping the tourism industry to make the best use of natural and cultural resources.

The success of this Pilot Green Tourism Accreditation Scheme will depend on the involvement of a representative sample of tourism businesses.

Its progress is being followed closely by the Tourist Board as it may be considered a suitable scheme for the whole of the country eventually. It is being financed by the three partnerships under the Natural Resource Rural Tourism initiative under the European Union Special Support Programme for Peace and Reconciliation.

You can find details of Northern Ireland's green initiative on www.nitb.com

Walkers and Cyclists Welcome Schemes

With the increasing emphasis on health, more and more people are taking active holidays. Walking and cycling comes high on the list of popular options. All over Britain walking and cycling routes have been and are still being set up, and visitors who enjoy these activities need to feel welcome when they arrive at their accommodation and throughout their stay. The necessary criteria for admission to schemes are not too difficult or expensive to meet and it is a worthwhile consideration to make a special point of welcoming both these visitors if you are located in the countryside.

England

The list of facilities and information provision necessary for admission to the Walkers and Cyclist schemes in England is fairly extensive, and you should contact the Quality Assurance department of VisitEngland or VisitBritain for the complete list of criteria, but some of the main points are as follows:

- separate space for drying outdoor clothing;

- a lockable shed or building for storage of bikes;

- access to a water point for washing cycles and outer garments;

- an emergency repair kit for punctures;

- a first aid kit;

- the possibility of pre-ordering basic groceries prior to arrival;

- details of the nearest cycle hire and repair shop;

- details of nearest doctor, dentist, hospital, all night chemist;

- maps and books (for reference) on cycling in the area with details of regional cycle routes, etc;

- information on local public transport and taxis with information about carriage facilities for bikes;

- weather information for the area or a telephone number for weather information;

- information on local attractions and events with directions and tourist information numbers;

- information on the nearest shops, bank or cash machine, telephone, post office, outdoor equipment shops (all with directions);

- local rescue numbers (mountain rescue, coastguard etc) with explanation for foreign visitors that the first number to contact is 999;

- details of the Countryside Code;

- information on other businesses in Walkers or Cyclist scheme.

Wales

Wales is an ideal country for walking and cycling, with open countryside and beautiful vistas and the opportunity to get away from the cities to the great outdoors. The Walkers and Cyclists schemes are very similar to the English ones with much the same criteria. For details of these schemes it is best to contact the Quality Assurance section of the Wales Tourist Board.

For each of the requirements necessary to be a member of the scheme there are also a number of best practices set out, e.g for self caterers to provide hot and cold drink making facilities (which any self catering property should of course have anyway). The suggestion is to provide an assortment of drinks such as a variety of teas (breakfast, decaffeinated, fruit teas), coffee (caffeinated and decaffeinated), hot chocolate, packet soups, squashes and cans. Fresh milk should also be available.

Scotland

Walking is the most popular activity undertaken by overseas and British visitors to Scotland, while cycling is an important growth area with an ever increasing number of cycle routes being developed in the countryside.

VisitScotland has worked with the Mountaineering Council of Scotland, Ramblers Association, Cyclists Touring Group and the Scottish Cyclists Union to provide two schemes to meet the specific accommodation needs of both walkers and cyclists.

You can choose to become a member of either the Walkers Welcome or the Cyclists Welcome scheme or both. To become a member of a scheme you must provide certain facilities and a VisitScotland Quality Advisor will inspect your property to verify that these facilities exist.

A full list of the criteria is available from VisitScotland but the sort of facilities you will need to provide as a self caterer are:

◆ a separate space for drying outdoor clothing and footwear at a sufficient temperature;

◆ information on location and opening times of the nearest shops and late-opening restaurants and pubs;

◆ information on local walks with maps if possible;

◆ local public transport information;

◆ telephone numbers for weather links and radio frequency and times for local weather forecasts;

- details of rescue services in the area;

- Ordnance Survey co-ordinates for the property if you are not in a village or town;

- clothes washing facilities or location of laundrette;

- information on local cycle routes (cyclists only);

- lockable storage shed for bikes (cyclists only);

- details of the nearest cycle specialist (cyclists only).

Northern Ireland

In Northern Ireland the scheme is being amended and details of the new requirements are not yet available (early 2005). You are therefore advised to check with the Northern Ireland Tourist Board for information. The website is www.nitb.com and other contact details are in the Appendix.

Disability Schemes

The Disability Rights Commission has issued an excellent booklet produced in partnership with representatives from the tourism industry and aimed specifically at all tourism accommodation owners. It explains very clearly their options under the Disability Discrimination Act (DDA) 1995. On 1 October 2004 the final part of this Act became law. This means that all businesses must make 'reasonable adjustments' to their premises or to the way they provide any services to ensure that they are not discriminating against those who are disabled.

It is usually assumed that being disabled means having mobility problems. It is not correct to pigeonhole people in such a narrow approach. In fact the DDA uses a broad definition of disability that embraces a far wider range of people:

- the blind or partially sighted;

- the deaf or hard of hearing;

- those with heart conditions;

- those with epilepsy;

- those who have problems with continence;

- those who are insulin dependent;

- people with Downs Syndrome;

- people with dyslexia;

- those with arthritis;

- wheelchair users;

- those with mental health problems;

- those with learning difficulties.

A fair proportion of your guests may already fall into these categories, possibly without you being aware of it.

Under the Act, even though you may only be a small business you are still expected to do as much as you reasonably can to make your cottages accessible to all visitors. There are certain measures which you might consider:

- making the printing on leaflets and brochures larger;

- allowing guide dogs and all assistance dogs access to your cottages;

- increasing the font size on your website (to 14 point sans serif);

- installing an induction loop in the sitting room;

- including a high backed chair in the sitting room;

- providing hand rails in a bathroom;

- providing a stool in a shower;

- creating clear colour contrasts between doors and walls.

There are very many more measures you can take and it might be worth checking with some of the schemes available on the tourism industry websites. They can provide guidance and suggestions for improvements you might not have thought about.

England

England has in place a National Accessibility Scheme, developed following extensive review with accommodation providers, guests and many organisations representing people with disabilities. The scheme provides a set of Accessible Standards against which establishments are assessed and awarded a rating. There are three sets of standards, covering three types of impairment, each with its own symbol:

♦ mobility;

♦ hearing;

♦ visual.

There are four categories for mobility, and two each for hearing and visual.

You can obtain details of all these from the Tourist Board on the industry website, or you can send for a pack. For level one you can carry out your own audit on all three standards (mobility, visual, hearing), using the NAS Self Survey. For any higher levels you will need to apply for individual Self Survey documents for the different standards. All can be downloaded from the website www.tourismtrade.org.uk.

Wales

A new National Accessibility Scheme is in development with criteria covering a wider range of disabilities than before. Wales has not yet adopted the new scheme as it is still in the consultancy stage, though the Tourist Board continues to encourage businesses to comply with the DDA by taking all reasonable steps to make their premises accessible to those with a disability.

The Tourist Board is not promoting the use of symbols to recommend facilities, as it feels that these on their own can be misinterpreted, but feels that a written access statement is the best way forward at present. By providing information in an Access Statement, the self caterer is seen as responding to the DDA.

This Statement should be an accurate description of the facilities and services that you provide – one that will enable a potential visitor to make a proper assessment as to whether your property(ies) will meet his or her needs. It can be presented in a variety of ways though the Tourist Board suggests a series of bullet points covering all the information required by a disabled person. This will be published on the Tourist Board website and should also be published on your website. Any brochure you have should also include this statement. There are fact sheets which should prove helpful, such as 'Designing visitor accommodation for disabled people', 'Providing facilities and services for disabled people' and 'What do guest accommodation providers need to know?'

Scotland

Scotland's Accessibility Assessment Quality Assurance Scheme is based on three categories of accessibility:

* unassisted wheelchair access;

* assisted wheelchair access;

* access for those with mobility problems.

As yet the Scottish Tourist Board has not developed a scheme which takes account of the fact that many disabilities are not connected with mobility. The requirements for category 1 (access for those with mobility problems) relate to accessibility for these guests in connection with the entrance to the property and the interior, with special reference to the bathrooms. For category 2 (assisted wheelchair access) you are required to make the building accessible to the passage of a wheelchair. The standards for the third category are more stringent. A Quality Assurance Assessor will inspect your premises in order to grade them to the correct standard.

Details of all these categories can be obtained by downloading them from the website www.scotexchange.net or by sending to VisitScotland.

Northern Ireland

Northern Ireland's National Accessible Scheme combines three sets of standards – mobility, hearing and visual – and was researched and developed by the English Tourism Council (ETC). When fully adopted, this scheme will enable visitors to make an informed choice of accommodation by using the rating system.

The Northern Ireland National Accessible Scheme mirrors closely the English scheme. Holiday cottage owners are encouraged to carry out an audit of their own premises for the different categories of impairment. Achieving the standards does not, however, guarantee compliance with the DDA. If you are building new holiday cottages they must comply with Part R of the Building Regulations (Northern Ireland) 2000 and you should also refer to the BS 8300-2001 Code of Practice.

Details of the National Scheme can be downloaded from the industry website www.nitb.com.

Check points

◆ There is an increasing emphasis on the environment. The various tourist boards have embraced this with a series of schemes aimed at the 'green' tourist. The major areas the initiatives cover are:
  – saving water;
  – saving energy;
  – reducing, re-using and re-cycling waste;
  – taking care with hazardous substances;
  – using greener transport;
  – planning and building sympathetically with the environment.

- VisitBritain runs a one-day Green Advantage Scheme which leads to a Certificate. Details of this scheme can be found on the industry website www.tourismtrade.org.uk.

- The Wales Tourist Board has issued a toolkit which lays out the principles of 'greener tourism' and helps businesses work towards the Green Dragon Standard. You can contact ARENA for details of this scheme (contact details in the Appendix).

- In Scotland a Green Tourism Business Scheme was established in 1998 by VisitScotland. It is an accredited Quality Assurance Scheme with gold, silver and bronze levels. For details contact the Green Tourism Business Scheme (see Appendix for contact details).

- Three tourism partnerships in Northern Ireland have joined forces to promote best environmental practice and sustainable tourism across their areas – Causeway Coast and Glens Heritage Trust, Mourne Heritage Trust and South Armagh Tourism Initiative – assisted by the Northern Ireland Tourist board. If proved successful, this Pilot Green Accreditation Scheme may be adopted across the country eventually. For details see www.nitb.com.

- Schemes encouraging walkers and cyclists are growing in popularity. England, Scotland and Wales all run such schemes. You can obtain full details from the tourism industry websites. In Northern Ireland the present scheme is in the process of amendment and details are not yet available.

- On 1 October 2004 the final part of the Disability Act came into force and businesses must now take 'all reasonable measures' to make their premises accessible to those with disabilities. The Disability Rights Commission has issued an excellent booklet 'What do guest accommodation owners need to know?' explaining the options for tourism businesses providing accommodation.

- The Disability Rights Commission sees disability as covering a far wider range than that previously considered. It encompasses those with mobility problems, mental health problems, those who are visually impaired, those who are hard of hearing etc.

◆ In England the National Accessibility Scheme covers the mobility, hearing and visual aspects of disability. Ratings are awarded on different levels, all audited by the owners of the properties themselves. Details of this scheme are on the industry website.

◆ Wales has not yet adopted the new scheme. At present, owners of accommodation are asked to provide an 'Access Statement' giving details of the accessibility of their properties. These statements should then be included on the owners' websites. Guidance details for writing the statement can be found on the industry website.

◆ Scotland has a Quality Assurance Scheme, based on the wheelchair logo with three levels. Your premises must be inspected by an Assessor to judge the level of access they merit. Details can be found on the industry website.

◆ Northern Ireland has three sets of standards – for mobility, visual and hearing, very similar to the scheme in England. These can be downloaded from the industry website.

PROGRESS PLAN

1. Consider which of the previous schemes (perhaps more than one) you would be interested in working towards. Carry out any necessary research by sending for the literature or by downloading it from the appropriate website and checking the criteria for the grade you hope to reach.

3. What do you still have to do to the properties to achieve this? Work out some costings for the changes you will have to make.

In conclusion

There are already many interesting graded schemes to attract visitors, available from the different Tourist Boards, and there will more in the years to come. Tourism in Britain is big business and, for it to remain so, we need increased numbers of tourists each year.

Some of these schemes are possibly not ideal for you, but there should be some that you can implement, if only in a small way. Complying with the Disability Act is a legal requirement but just how far you can go to meet its demand of 'reasonable measures' is a very individual decision for you to make.

Check the National Tourist Board sites frequently for any update on these schemes and keep in touch with other self caterers to see how they are dealing with the very different demands of all these initiatives.

12

Tourism Organisations

Tourism organisations, bodies and associations can prove very useful to you as a self caterer. The self catering industry does not exist in a vacuum and it is only sensible to be aware of the business advice, marketing initiatives and networking opportunities that these organisations can bring. It is very easy to concentrate so much on building up your own business that everything else is excluded including the ideas and assistance which might benefit you from outside your own immediate field of self catering. It is definitely worth considering joining a self catering association for all the help, encouragement and back-up they can provide as well as being able to talk to people who have the same problems and the same enthusiasms as you. Contact details for all of the following bodies are included in the Appendix.

UK wide

The Federation of National Self-Catering Associations (FONSCA)

The following are members of FONSCA: the English Association of Self-Catering Operators, the Welsh Association of Self Catering Operators, the Northern Ireland Self-Catering Holiday Association and the Association of Scotland's Self-Caterers.

The Federation of Small Businesses

The FBS is a non-party, UK wide, political pressure group that promotes and protects the interests of all who own and/or manage small and medium sized businesses. The FSB also responds to consultation documents ensuring that the voice of the small business proprietor is heard. It is also represented on a number of public bodies.

FBS provides members with a wide range of benefits including a useful and free legal helpline and advice for any in-depth investigations by the Inland Revenue and Customs and Excise.

England

Tourism in England is based on the National Tourist Board (see previous chapter), the Regional Tourist Boards, VisitBritain partnerships and the various trade organisations in the private sector.

Regional Tourist Boards

At a local level there are 17 Regional Tourist Boards, each covering an area of England including the Isle of Man and the Channel Islands. These are:

◆ Cheshire and Warrington Tourism Board.

◆ Cumbria Tourist Board, covering Cumbria and The Lake District.

- East Midlands Tourism, covering Derbyshire, Nottingham, Lincolnshire, Leicestershire, Rutland and Northamptonshire.

- East of England Tourist Board, covering Bedfordshire, Cambridgeshire, Essex, Hertfordshire, Norfolk and Suffolk.

- England's North Country, an Overseas Marketing Consortium of Cumbria, North West, Northumbria, Yorkshire, Isle of Man Tourist Boards and Manchester Airport.

- Heart of England Tourism, covering Herefordshire, Shropshire, Staffordshire, Warwickshire, Worcestershire and the West Midlands.

- Isle of Man Tourism.

- Jersey Tourism.

- Lancashire and Blackpool Tourist Board.

- Marketing Manchester.

- One NorthEast Tourism Team, covering Northumberland, Tyne and Wear, County Durham and the Tees Valley.

- South West Tourism, covering Bath, Bristol, Cornwall, Gloucestershire, Isles of Scilly, Devon, Dorset, Somerset and Wiltshire.

- The Mersey Partnership.

- Tourism South East, covering Berkshire, Buckinghamshire, East Sussex, Hampshire, Isle of Wight, Kent, Oxfordshire, Surrey and West Sussex.

- VisitGuernsey, covering Guernsey, Sark, Alderney, Herm and Libou and the other smaller islands.

- Visit London.

- Yorkshire Tourist Board, covering East Riding of Yorkshire, North East Lincolnshire, North, South and West Yorkshire and North Lincolnshire.

The British Tourism Development Committee (BTDC)

The BTDC was set up in 1995 by BDA to act as a statutory forum for discussion and representation to government, VisitBritain and the other statutory Tourist Boards, and public and private sector organisations on all matters affecting the tourist industry in Britain.

Members of the Committee include the AA, the British Hospitality Association, the British Resorts Association, the British Tourism Partnership, The Federation of National Self-Catering Associations and the English Association of Self-Catering operators.

The Tourism Alliance

The Tourism Alliance is a body that works to establish and maintain a favourable operating environment for all businesses involved in tourism, particularly in England. It lobbies the government in Britain and in Brussels on the key issues facing the industry. Its members, comprising trade associations and trade bodies, include Cumbria and Lakeland Self Caters Association as well as several regional tourist boards. The Alliance is supported by the Confederation of British Industry (CBI).

Trade associations

◆ **The Cumbria and Lakeland Self Caterers Association (CaLS-CA)**. CaLSCA is a trade association of independent self catering providers in Cumbria and the Lakes area. It has a property inspection scheme recognised by the Cumbria Tourist Board and all the local authorities and operates a website which allows visitors to search for properties and availability online. For its members there are newsletters and meetings to keep them informed of developments in the industry.

◆ **The English Association of Self-Catering Operators (EASCO)**. This is the co-ordinated national voice of self catering operators throughout England. It represents small and medium sized businesses which provide self catering holiday accommodation in houses, apartments, cottages, log cabins, etc.

As part of its remit to encourage and promote high standards across the country, it liaises with government departments and with national and regional tourism bodies as the voice of the self catering industry in England.

Member benefits include:

- a property listing on the website;
- password access to a members only section on the site;
- a tailor-made insurance scheme at a very competitive rate for property owners;
- special rates for credit card business facilities;
- a tax and accountancy service from Tax Watchdog;
- holiday cancellation insurance;
- private health care insurance;
- discounts on tyres, exhausts and batteries;
- discounted rates on telephone calls.

The Association works to gain recognition of the important role self catering plays in tourism today and to keep members abreast of any relevant developments in the industry. EASCO is the only nationwide trade association for providers of self catering accommodation in England and as such is a very useful organisation that you should consider joining.

The membership also includes self catering cottage agencies and local associations of self caterers.

Wales

There are many organisations and bodies involved in tourism in Wales. Some of the most relevant here are the Wales Tourist Board (see previous chapter), the regional tourism partnerships, the local authorities and the membership organisations.

Regional Tourism Partnerships

Four Regional Tourism Partnerships (RTPs) were set up in 2002 in order to lead the implementation of four regional tourism strategies which seek to improve the competitive performance of tourism so that it makes a better contribution to the economic and social prosperity of

Wales. The RTPs work in partnership with the Wales Tourist Board, local authorities, tourism businesses and with other organisations to undertake a range of marketing, investment and business support activities on behalf of the tourism industry. Most of these activities will be delivered under contract by third parties. The Wales Tourist Board is devolving a greater level of funding to the RTPs to support the activities they deliver, and is working closely with them to ensure that resources are used effectively.

+ **North Wales Tourism Partnership**. Tourism brings in £595 million to the economy in north Wales and the role of this partnership is to ensure that this figure continues to grow by capitalising on the area's unique appeal and character.

+ **Mid Wales Tourism Partnership**. Tourism currently contributes £298 million to the mid Wales economy and is a vital employer in the region.

+ **South West Wales Tourism Partnership**. The south western region of Wales consists of some of the best coastal scenery in the UK, as well as great swathes of inland pastureland. Tourism currently contributes £477 million to the south west Wales economy.

+ **Capital Region Tourism Partnership**. This partnership's region is the most urban of the four and includes the capital city Cardiff. Currently tourism brings in £436 million to the area. The challenge is to capitalise on Cardiff's current success in attracting big name events, and extend the benefits further afield, developing the region into a true gateway to the rest of Wales.

Local Authorities

All Local and National Park Authorities, to varying degrees, play a significant role in the promotion of the tourism product in Wales. Although not one of the local authorities statutory responsibilities, many of these authorities recognise tourism as a key economic driver in their area and therefore are actively involved in the industry.

Membership organisations

There are many membership organisations in the tourism industry in Wales. Their role is to represent their members' interests in order to ensure that the voice of the industry is heard on key issues and to advise the Wales Tourist Board.

◆ **Wales Tourism Alliance**. The Wales Tourism Alliance, formed in 2002, aims to link sectors and raise main policy matters with politicians and the Wales Tourist Board. The membership is made up of national and regional tourism-led organisations from the whole of the country, including the Federation of Small Businesses, the Wales Association of Self Catering Operators, Mid Wales Tourism, North Wales Tourism and the South West Wales Tourism Associations.

◆ **Wales Association of Self Catering Operators (WASCO)**. In 1994 the Wales Tourist Board convened a Wales National Self Catering Conference. The meeting voted in favour of the formation of a trade organisation to represent their interests. The Wales Association of Self Catering Operators was launched in 1995.

Membership is open to any person or organisation who owns, manages or lets holiday accommodation (other than tents or caravans) in Wales. Members must have applied to participate in the Wales Tourist Board's grading scheme within one year of joining.

Benefits of membership include:

- Campaigning to gain rightful recognition of the holiday cottage industry, as Wales's most successful accommodation sector.
- Representation as the voice of the industry on leading tourism groups and organisations, including the Wales Tourism Alliance, the Regional Tourism Companies, the Wales Tourist Board UK Marketing Focus group and the Federation of National Self Catering Associations.
- Consultation in an attempt to achieve the best results for the members, for example details in the new grading scheme for self catering were framed by a joint WTB/WASCO working party.
- Newsletters, meetings and conferences.
- The opportunity to advertise properties on the association website.

> – Membership discounts for advertising with Stilwells Cottage Guide.
> – Discounts for taking out insurance, both for the properties and for holiday insurance, through the recommended broker.
> This body is arguably the most directly relevant to self catering businesses in Wales.

◆ **Local Tourism Associations**. Tourism Associations are groups of local tourism business people who have come together to form Tourism Associations to promote tourism in their local community. There are associations for each of the 12 marketing areas in Wales.
  – Isle of Anglesey.
  – Llandudno, Colwyn Bay, Rhyl and Prestatyn.
  – The North Wales Borderlands.
  – Snowdonia Mountains and Coast.
  – Mid Wales and Brecon Beacons.
  – Ceredigion (Cardigan Bay).
  – Pembrokeshire.
  – Carmarthenshire (the Garden of Wales).
  – Swansea Bay (Gower, Mumbles and Afan and the Vale of Neath).
  – Valleys of South Wales.
  – Cardiff (Glamorgan Heritage Coast and Countryside).
  – Wye Valley and the Vale of Usk.

◆ **Mid Wales Tourism (MWT)**. Mid Wales Tourism, a company limited by guarantee, was formed in 1991. MWT is the main deliverer of support for the tourism industry in mid Wales i.e. Powys, Ceredigion and the Meirionnydd area of Gwynedd.
  It is the main membership organisation for all tourism businesses in mid Wales and has about 700 members. Benefits include free listing on the regional website, preferential banking facilities, and rates for credit card processing, discounts on specialist insurance, leaflet distribution and provision of discount vouchers towards training courses.

◆ **North Wales Tourism (NWT)**. NWT represents over 1,300 private sector and public institutions within the North Wales tourism/ hospitality industry. It is the principal deliverer of support for the tourism industry on a partnership basis.

◆ **South West Wales Tourism Associations (SWWTA)**. The four local tourism associations of South West Wales (Carmarthenshire Tourist Association, Pembrokeshire Tourism, Tourism Swansea, and Neath and Port Talbot Tourism) provide the tourism and hospitality industry of South West Wales with organisations which the trade owns and directs, and which participate in the partnership delivery of local, regional and national strategies.

They now work with South West Wales Tourism Partnership, the WDA, the county councils of the region and regional facilitators to encourage tourists to the region through marketing area brochures and web sites.

◆ **Association of Welsh Agents (AWA)**. Self catering agents that had previously participated in the WTB grading scheme decided to form an Association of Welsh Agents and to become members of the Wales Tourism Alliance to facilitate communication between the agents themselves, the WTB and the WTA.

The Association includes virtually all the Wales based agents (and one just over the border in England). Its members represent in the region of 2,500 self catering units.

Scotland

Many bodies, both public and private, are involved in working to help make tourism the number one industry in Scotland, vital to the country's economy.

At the local level three main bodies have significant impact on the industry.

◆ **The Integrated Tourism Network**. This has replaced the original Area Tourist Boards throughout Scotland. The decision was made to set up a new network of 14 tourism hubs integrated with VisitScotland. Each hub is accountable to VisitScotland and has the responsibility for the delivery of the national tourism strategy in its area. The separate areas covered are the same as with the original ATBs:

– Aberdeen and Grampian;

– Angus and Dundee;

– Argyll, the Isles, Loch Lomond, Stirling and the Trossachs;

– Ayrshire and Arran;

– Dumfries and Galloway;

– Edinburgh and the Lothians;

– Greater Glasgow and the Clyde Valley;

– Highlands of Scotland;

– Kingdom of Fife;

– Orkney;

– Perthshire;

– Scottish Borders;

– Shetland;

– Western Isles.

Businesses no longer need to pay membership fees but can buy into as many as they wish of many commercial packages on offer.

As part of this Network there is close integration of services with the enterprise companies and with the local authorities (see below). The Network sets up partnerships in each area supported by the Tourism Network office and with strong representation from local authorities and businesses. These partnerships are responsible for developing area tourism partnership plans.

♦ **Local Enterprise Companies**. There are at present 22 Local Enterprise Companies (LECs) operating in Scotland – ten under the Highlands and Islands Enterprise and 12 under Scottish Enterprise.

♦ **Local authorities**. Local authorities play a role in tourism. Through partnerships with the local tourism businesses and the Integrated Tourism Network (see above), they provide funding for developing area tourism partnership plans.

At national level there are two official agencies working for the promotion of tourism in Scotland as well as the National Tourist Board (see previous chapter):

♦ **Scottish Enterprise (SE)**. The Scottish Enterprise Network consists of Scottish Enterprise National, based in Glasgow, and 12 Local Enterprise Companies stretching from Grampian to the Borders. SE is funded through the Scottish Executive's Department of Enterprise and

Lifelong Learning. The main aim of the organisation is to work with businesses and people in the private sector as well as with public bodies in order to contribute financially to projects which are of economic benefit to the country. Tourism is a large part of this planned activity. In this area SE can help with tourism business start-ups as well as any training necessary to make your business a success.

Scottish Enterprise works in conjunction with Business Gateway to advise businesses on various relevant topics. They will provide factsheets on what you need to know about starting up and are available for advice.

◆ **Highlands and Islands Enterprise (HIE)**. Highlands and Islands Enterprise, based in Inverness, is responsible for delivering economic and community development services through a network of the ten local enterprise companies. As with SE, HIE is funded through the Scottish Executive's Department of Enterprise and Lifelong Learning. Assisting with the development of quality tourism in the Highlands is recognised as the key to realising the full potential of the area. HIE exists to help growing businesses with the aid of financial assistance, advice, training and marketing. There is also support for community based projects such as local festivals and events – which also encourages tourism in the different areas.

There are also several partnerships, forums and trade associations involving private and/or public sector bodies:

◆ **Tourism agencies**. There are many other agencies involved in tourism in some way in Scotland. These range from Historic Scotland, the Scottish Museums Council, Sportscotland, etc to the Forestry Commission. Private sector involvement is present in the Scottish Tourism Forum (see below), an agency which has both public and private sector representation.

Worth a mention is the Tourism and Environment Forum. Recent research on the attitudes of visitors in Scotland shows that the environment is the country's number one asset. Scenery, wildlife and nature were in the top five attributes that visitors associated with Scotland. The landscape or countryside was the most important factor in determining their visit. The Forum works to carry out market research, to promote environmental best practices and to encourage an integrated approach to tourism and the environment.

◆ **Association of Scotland's Self-Caterers (ASSC).** This is the most directly relevant association for self caterers. Formed in 1978, the ASSC is the only trade body representing owners and operators of self catering businesses in Scotland, with holiday properties ranging from cottages and chalets to flats, lodges and castles.

Members can be owners of single properties, operators making a full or second income from their holiday home business, owners who let their properties through agencies and operators of large self catering complexes (but not static caravans). The membership also includes self catering cottage agencies and local associations of self caterers.

Membership details are available on the website (see Appendix).

By joining the ASSC you will gain the following benefits:

– the right to use the ASSC logo;
– representation of your interests with VisitScotland and its Quality and Standards Scheme, with visitscotland.com, with the Federation of National Self-Catering Associations and the Local Enterprise Companies;
– pressure on central and local government, lobbying on behalf of self catering and acting as a watchdog;
– advice and news relevant to self catering, through the regular newsletter and guidance notes on topics such as rates, terms of letting, meeting your VisitScotland Quality and Standards advisors, licensing, fire regulations and others;
– online members' notice board;
– marketing support through the ASSC website;
– benefit through discounts in leading tourism publications;
– opportunity to advertise in the full-colour directory for the ASSC;
– opportunities for meetings and making contacts;
– free helpline for legal advice from a team of specialist lawyers;
– free helpline for tax queries through an approved firm of accountants;

- a single point of contact for enquiries on energy and the environment;
- custom-made insurance policies at keen rates for self caterers covering buildings, contents, public liability and cancellation;
- recommended specialist suppliers to the trade.

◆ **Tourism Innovation Group (TIG)**. The stated purpose of this group is to innovate, lead, inspire and drive forward Scottish tourism. The Group was formed in 2002 as an industry driven partnership of business leaders and public agencies. They are seeking new and exciting ways to reverse any decline in tourism. They are working on several projects including the promotion of examples of best practice, improvements in customer focus and in tourist provision, for example the encouragement of traditional music in pubs. They also are interested in promoting festivals such as those connected with food and drink and local culture.

◆ **Scottish Tourism Forum**. The Scottish Tourism Forum comprises tourism trade associations, businesses, marketing and local area tourism groups which earn their living from tourism or have an active interest in tourism. The Forum works to unite all tourism interests with effective and independent communication and lobbying. In recognising the importance of tourism to the country, their aim is to contribute to the strengthening of Scottish tourism. At present there are 20,000 tourism businesses in Scotland, generating £4.5 billion for the country per annum.

The Forum produces a newsletter and holds meetings at which all members are welcome. They provide a useful networking opportunity. Self catering cannot exist on its own but has to be part of a wider industry. The meetings give you an opportunity to talk to people in forestry, touring, national parks, etc.

Northern Ireland

Over and above the main tourist board for the country (see previous chapter), among Northern Ireland's tourism partners that might be relevant to you as a self caterer are some of the regional tourism organisations, the government bodies and an accommodation organisation.

Regional tourism organisations (RTOs)

◆ **Derry Visitor and Convention Bureau**. This is the regional tourism organisation for the City of Derry and the North West. It is a membership organisation and has two key roles – marketing and visitor servicing. The emphasis at present is to encourage short breaks and to develop the city as a destination for business tourism.

◆ **Kingdoms of Down (KOD)**. This RTO represents over 400 members from the Ards, Down, Lisburn and the North Down local authority areas. Its main emphasis is on a 'product approach', e.g. heritage, homes and gardens, equestrian, angling and walking.

◆ **Causeway Coast and Glens (CCAG)**. This is responsible for tourism marketing in the areas of Ballymena, Ballymoney, Carrickfergus, Coleraine, Larne, Limavady, Moyle and Newtownabbey. Over 400 businesses are represented here from the complete range of tourism sectors. CCAG works in association with the Causeway Coast and Glens Heritage Trust which is responsible for natural and sustainable tourism.

◆ **Belfast Visitor and Convention Bureau (BVCB)**. This RTO was established in 1999 to promote Belfast as a major leisure and business destination. It represents over 300 businesses in the Greater Belfast area and manages the Belfast Tourist Information Centre.

◆ **Fernmanagh Lakeland Tourism (FLT)**. FLT's role is to promote Fermanagh as the country's top natural lakeland and waterway destination. It represents over 350 members in the Fermanagh local authority area in marketing, undertaking marketing campaigns in particular areas.

◆ **Sperrins Tourism**. Sperrins Tourism Limited was established in 1999 as a partnership body with equal representation at board level from the public sector (50%) and from private/community/voluntary sectors (50%). Membership totals 148 accommodation providers, activity providers, restaurants, visitor attractions, craft workers and other individuals and organisations.

This regional agency is responsible for the development of tourism in the Sperrins region and the marketing of the region – the entire

District Council areas of Cookstown, Magherafelt, Omagh and Strabane as well as adjacent wards in Derry, Limavady and Coleraine local authority areas.

Government bodies

◆ **Invest NI**. Invest NI was established in 2002 to continue the functions carried out previously by a number of boards and units such as the Local Enterprise Development Unit, the business support functions of the NI Tourist Board and the Business Support Division of the Department of Enterprise, Trade and Investment. It encourages innovation and entrepreneurship.

◆ **The Department of Enterprise Trade and Investment (DETI)**. DETI is responsible for economic policy development, energy tourism, health and safety at work, etc. It has four agencies established as public bodies, one of which is the Northern Ireland Tourist Board.

Accommodation organisations

◆ **Rural Cottage Holidays.** This is the only specialist holiday home organisation that has a dedicated booking desk Monday to Friday. They emphasise that this is a real advantage in bolstering your own bookings round the year.

The company markets about 200 cottages, holiday homes and apartments throughout Northern Ireland and the Border Counties of the Republic, a large percentage of which appear on their website and in the brochure which has a wide distribution. Their commission is currently 15%.

◆ **NI Self Catering Holidays Association (NISCHA)**. The Association was founded in 1989, when 16 self catering property owners came together to form a marketing consortium with the aspiration of growing to act as the representative body for the self catering industry in Northern Ireland.

Since that date membership has grown considerably and the Association is now recognised by the Northern Ireland Tourist Board as the nationwide representative body for the self catering sector.

Membership is open to any person or organisation who owns, manages or lets holiday accommodation (other than caravans or tents) in Northern Ireland and whose property has been inspected and has received an NITB Quality Assurance star rating.

The benefits of membership include:

- representation of your interests to NITB and government agencies, Area Tourist Boards and the Federation of Self Catering Associations;
- consultation to achieve best results for members;
- advice and news through regular newsletters;
- negotiated member discounts including reduced costs for advertising and insurance when you cover property and liabilities through the recommended broker;
- meetings with other self caterers;
- participation in joint marketing activities which include an annual brochure and advertising on the Association's website. There are also invitations to participate in special promotions in key market campaigns.

PROGRESS PLAN

Start to select those bodies and organisations involved in tourism that are going to be useful to you in your business.

1. Which particular organisations seem worth following up? Check the websites of any which you are interested in both from a direct business point of view and from a more personal angle.

2. Get some idea of the cost involved in joining these various groups and schemes – have you included this in your business plan?

3. Does some of your intended advertising depend on you having paid to join a particular group or scheme? Establish the details.

In conclusion

Many of these groups and associations will prove of interest to you as a self caterer and as a member of the tourist industry. It is worth keeping an eye on developments in tourism and to be aware of any marketing initiatives you might be able to take part in or benefit from. These may not be exclusively designed for self catering but will have an impact on your branch of the industry nevertheless.

You may have already made up your mind which associations or bodies you intend to join, but you should have a look at any that seem relevant to your country and area. Their websites give a good indication of where they stand on issues and will help you decide how many of them are relevant to your business and to your future.

Keep checking on these websites as they are a source of new information, being regularly updated.

In many cases it is not necessary to become a member to benefit from the advice and assistance they can provide.

Part Two
Making a Success of Your Business

13

Marketing and Advertising

Correct marketing is essential to your business. You might have the most beautiful cottages, well equipped and in a superb location, but the way you market those cottages is crucial in determining whether your business is successful or not.

You have already decided on the type of visitor you want to attract. How will you reach this visitor? How will you present your properties in any advertisement? If for example, you want to attract families you will need to be able to reach this market and persuade them that you can provide the ideal holiday for both parents and children. Equally, for walkers and climbers you need to be situated in the right area and convince them that you are sympathetic to their needs and happy to cater for them.

First consider what your strategy is to be. Do you intend to market your property yourself or to work through an agency, either exclusively or for a certain numbers of weeks per year?

There is a good argument for drawing up a plan specifically for marketing your business. It need not be complicated or lengthy, but it will help you to focus your mind on the main issues.

Your plan obviously needs to be visitor orientated. After all, the whole point of the exercise is to attract a constant stream of people to your accommodation and encourage some percentage of them to return, as often as possible.

Some of the national tourism industry websites offer advice on marketing your business, and though it is understandably biased towards the Tourist Boards themselves, there are useful tips which can be applied to any situation.

Agencies

There are very many commercial holiday cottage agencies only too happy to manage your property for you. They will market it and deal with the bookings. You will still have the cleaning, maintenance and the looking after of the visitors of course, but it certainly removes some of the pressure from you. Most of these agencies are happy to deal with bookings, either in total or for a stipulated number of weeks during the year. It is up to you to decide which, and how many weeks. They normally charge a fee of about 20% per booking, so a proportion of owners raise their weekly prices accordingly, although this can be risky as it may price them out of the market for a lot of people.

Your property will be advertised through the agency, probably on the internet and by brochure. You can see any number of these agencies in the travel section of the Sunday newspapers or in the advertising section at the end of magazines. Once you start up in business you will receive invitations to join these agencies by letter and by email. If you want to do this, then check the small print carefully and ask around to see if you can find any other holiday cottage owner who works through them. Are they satisfied with the response they get through the agency and do they consider them to be a real benefit?

Apart from these large commercial companies there are the smaller more personal agencies, possibly managed by a cottage owner, who will take on similar holiday cottages in the area. Again, check the terms and conditions and speak to other owners dealing with that agency. Find out how they advertise and what percentage of the weekly booking fee they charge.

Whether you decide to go it alone or to use an agency for part of the year only, you will have to find out how to reach your target market. This needs a bit of lateral thinking on occasion as you want to make sure you have explored all the avenues but used only the really relevant forms of advertising. Placing an advertisement is expensive and you cannot afford to waste too much money on unsuccessful attempts to attract your visitor.

How to reach your visitor – an example

If you intend to market your property to walkers and climbers, for example, how will you reach them? If you are a climber yourself this is relatively easy as you will know the market, but if you are new to the whole business, then it is more difficult. Check the newsagents – they will have magazines dedicated to this field. Go into outdoor clothing shops – they too will have magazines on show. Note the more popular magazines and buy one or two of them. Look at the sections featuring accommodation. Is this the sort of advertising you want to do? Is there enough advertising of the right sort? If so, check the costs of the different size and style of the advertisements available.

In some of these magazines you may see further useful areas for advertising mentioned. The John Muir Trust, for example, owns large tracts of land in Britain which it conserves for the Trust and makes available to walkers. They hold meetings and discussions and joining the Trust both enables you to advertise your accommodation in their annual booklet, reaching the right market, and to keep abreast of developments in the countryside.

The different National Tourist Boards have schemes you can join called Walkers Welcome or Walkers and Cyclists. You will need to provide certain facilities (see Chapter 11) and pay to be inspected, but being able to use the logo is a useful 'hook' to those interested in this field.

In your advertisement make it clear that not only do you welcome walkers and climbers, but you go to some effort to provide the right sort of facilities, and that both the area and the cottage are not only suitable but perfect for them. Consider advertising short breaks too as these are popular with many climbers who want to visit for a long weekend possibly in the winter months.

In your own brochure and on your website you would make a point of stressing that you have good facilities for walkers. Mention the names of some of the natural features of the country round about your property, especially if it is known as an area of special interest to walkers.

If you can find websites dedicated to walkers and climbers, find out if you can feature your property on them or at least pay for a link to your own website from their site.

Advertising

It is important to establish a budget for advertising and stick to it. Advertising is an essential tool but you should try to keep costs down as much as possible. Some advertising is very expensive, but may be also very effective – you will not be able to tell at the beginning. The first year or so will be difficult as you cannot possibly know in advance which publications will work for you. You will be making all your decisions largely by trial and error initially.

Whatever your market there are certain directions open to you for advertising:

+ your own website;
+ commercial websites;
+ newspapers;
+ magazines;
+ brochures;
+ business cards and stationery;
+ the Tourist Board.

Your own website

Having your own website is essential for any tourism business nowadays. Increasingly, people want to book their holidays, both at home and abroad, on the internet. In order to compete you need a good website, with clear information and images.

If you are confident about setting up your own site there are software packages such as Microsoft Frontpage which will guide you through the set-up. There are also many useful books on the subject or you could just save the pages of a website you particularly admire and learn the HTML coding from that, adapting it to your own use.

On the other hand, there are many commercial companies offering website design and it is perhaps better to buy in expertise in this field than try to build your own site. If you are not too concerned about employing a local company, check through some of the better individual websites in any commercial holiday cottage business website. Choose one or two that you are really impressed with. The designers' names are often to be found somewhere on the page. Or go by word of mouth. If you have moved to an area, ask around some of the local businesses that have impressive websites. You will soon hear if they are happy with the web designer or not.

There are two main methods the designer can use. They can either customise a package, adapting it to the particular needs of your business, or design a new website for you from scratch. The second is the more expensive option, as the designer will have to spend much more time on the project and the cost has to reflect this.

You will need a web name. Registers such as www.Networksolutions.com can provide you with a name – choose one that reflects your accommodation business. Alternatively, if you employ a web designer they may also be able to provide you with a name as can many Internet Service Providers. Your business property name should be at the heart of this web address – this will make it more likely to be picked up by the search engines. Do not forget to set up corresponding email addresses for the business.

Your website should provide:

♦ Initial positive impact.

♦ An attractive home page with fast links to the other pages in your website.

♦ Efficient links between the pages and to other websites such as castles, activities, tourist attractions, etc.

♦ Clear and attractive images of the properties, inside and out.

♦ A short description of the rooms and facilities in the properties, highlighting any particular features.

♦ Directions to your properties, possibly with a map.

♦ Prices and what is included (and what is not).

♦ The facility to advertise any special offers.

♦ A short description of the surrounding area.

♦ Mention of any activities in the area such as fishing, water sports, etc.

♦ A list of particular features or buildings of interest in the area such as stately homes, towns of note, wildlife parks, etc.

♦ The nearest places to eat, shop, etc.

♦ Terms and conditions of booking.

- Cancellation charges.

- Good visibility to search engines.

You might also like to consider including:

- Special events in the area such as food festivals, Highland Games, boat races, etc.

- Availability calendar for each property.

- Possible online booking facility.

- Translations into different languages.

Your website should also be easily maintained, either by you or the designer at a reasonable cost. The designer will make a yearly hosting charge.

It is essential that your website is picked up by all the major search engines. Unfortunately everyone with a business website thinks the same and there is a vast number of sites competing for attention. So not only do you need to ensure you are picked up but you must feature on the first couple of pages of the search results. If you use a commercial company for this, make sure they use key words and phrases in the text and the titles that you feel are appropriate for your business. There are also companies which will present your website to the major search engines on a regular basis or when necessary. If you set up in business they will probably contact you.

Commercial websites

New commercial websites for accommodation are springing up every year. You cannot advertise on all of them and it pays to be selective. Many new sites offer free advertising for the first six months or even a year. It does no harm to take advantage of this, but when it comes to the time for payment you need to assess just how useful the website has been for you.

Most sites offer different rates of advertising, often with general pages featuring all the properties in an area, with a 'click through' facility to the page dedicated to your property with pictures and text. Many will also offer a link through to your own website. This is very worth while paying for. The commercial site is not an alternative to having your own website. Some sites offer booking forms so that when you get an enquiry or a booking you can see where it originated. There is also downloadable software available that can give you this information, both about the number of hits you receive on your site and where those hits come from.

Some of the sites are for general accommodation – for hotels, guest houses, B&Bs, as well as holiday cottages. Some are dedicated to holiday cottages only and these are the most effective ones to use. Asking other holiday cottage owners will also give you an idea of the most useful ones.

Before advertising take a good look at the possibilities. You are looking for a website with clear images and accurate information. It should have a wide range of properties (therefore popular) – check those you know to be in the area round you – with links to the individual cottages. Does it go further, giving a list of visitor attractions or tourist facilities in the area? These are not strictly necessary but a bonus for the viewer if they are both correct and reasonably comprehensive. There is one more essential ingredient for these sites – they should rate highly on the main search engines.

To find some of these sites, enter a string of likely words such as 'holiday cottages in the Highlands' or 'cottages in Cornwall' into a search engine. Use the words you think any prospective visitor might use. From the list that comes up on the screen you can spot the best accommodation websites – they will feature near the beginning of the first page.

There are also websites that are dedicated to the particular interests of some visitors – motor cyclists, walkers or dog owners, for example.

Whatever you choose, keep a check on its usefulness and take this into consideration before paying for a further year's subscription.

Newspapers

Some accommodation providers will swear by newspaper advertising and some never use it. It is a form of advertising which does not require you to book long in advance. If you have some availability in your properties during a particular few weeks it is possible to try advertising in a newspaper at the last moment. Sunday papers are probably better than dailies, perhaps because most people have more time to read them.

As part of your marketing strategy, pick your newspaper wisely. If you are going for the top end of the market then choose accordingly – likewise for the family market. On top of the basic text, you will have to decide whether you think the extra cost of a picture is necessary. Check the other advertisements and see which you think looks the most effective. Make sure all the necessary detail is included. It is easy to miss out some vital fact such as:

- name of establishment;
- what it is, i.e. self catering cottages, lodges, etc;
- where it is;
- contact details, i.e. telephone number, email address, website.

If there are any special features such as log fires, nearby national park, skiing or children's activities, for example, then mention these as well.

Always check the proofs thoroughly to make sure all the details are accurate. An incorrect phone number, for example, can ruin the effectiveness of your advert.

◆ TOP TIP ◆

Newspaper advertising is mostly used in addition to a longer term advertising campaign, and as such can provide a useful boost to bookings in a quiet period.

Magazines

We find magazine advertising very useful for reaching the niche market. There are magazines for practically everything nowadays, from houses to pets and from gardens to steam railways. Have a look on any newsagent's shelf and you will find an incredible range of publications.

Whichever market you pick, check in the magazine first to see if accommodation is well represented. You would be wise to choose one in which self catering itself is featured. Motor cyclist magazines for example rarely feature holiday cottages and for a very good reason. The motor cyclist usually wants to move on constantly on holiday, so a hotel, guest house or B&B is far more suitable for them.

Check advertising rates and the number of issues a year. These vary widely. Do you want to advertise in every issue or at certain times of the year? Do you want to include a picture? On the down side, once you do advertise with any publication, the sales staff will phone you at regular intervals ever afterwards. Also, rival publications will contact you, having seen your original advertisement. In spite of this magazines are a very good method of getting a stream of enquiries for your business from the very people you are trying to attract.

The same rules apply to this as for newspaper advertising (see previous bullet list). Also include any special offer you are making or particular feature of the property which will make it stand out from the norm.

As well as the niche markets, there are magazines such as those for the cross-Channel ferries, notably that for the Rosyth-Zeebrugge route. This is a very upmarket publication though, having tried it, I am not sure of its effectiveness for the self catering market.

There are also the specialised publications dedicated to holiday cottages or self catering. These are usually published annually but can sometimes be issued more frequently, on a monthly or quarterly basis. They provide a very useful form of advertising but are sometimes quite expensive. You will see these magazines on the shelves of the main newsagents and supermarkets. You could always try them for a year and see what you think.

Lastly there are the general magazines, some of them very well known, such as those with 'home', 'gardens', the 'countryside' etc in the titles. Advertising in these tends to be very expensive.

Brochures

Many people feel that the world has moved on with the introduction of the internet and the possibilities of websites. It has, but there is still a place for paper communication in the form of a brochure. Not everyone has a computer and even if they have, the brochure is still a popular source of information.

Brochures can be professionally produced or you can create your own on the computer very easily with the aid of a software package such as Microsoft Publisher, a scanner or digital camera and a good printer. Printing your own brochure means that you can print as many as you need when you need them and you can amend the details anytime.

Having brochures professionally printed may make them look better, but you may have a large number of brochures that you cannot amend if some detail about the area or the properties, or even your email address, changes. Consider printing your accommodation prices separately as these will obviously change yearly. They can be included as an insert if you wish. When you get towards the autumn months, enquirers could be asking about prices for that year and/or the next.

Your brochure should look as professional as possible even if you produce it yourself. It should feature:

- The name of the establishment.
- A clear picture of the property/properties.
- A general description of the property and immediate area.
- A description of each type of property (if they differ) and possibly pictures.
- Prices (on a separate insert).

- Details of the facilities with any special features such as a log fire or jacuzzi.

- Particular features in the area, such as mountain views, lake, peaceful location, etc.

- Full contact details – address with postcode, telephone number, email address, website, fax number (if applicable).

- Clear directions to reach the properties.

- Details of levels of disability for which you cater.

You might also include:

- A short description of the wider area with possible touring destinations.

- Activities in the area such as boat trips, leisure centres, extreme sports, etc.

- Special features within easy reach, e.g stately homes, castles, national parks, theme parks, etc.

- Local wildlife.

- A plan of the layout of the cottage(s).

There will be considerable wastage with these brochures. This is unavoidable, as people will often send for three or four brochures from different properties when choosing their holiday. Think of it as an investment – after all, if they do not visit you this year they may come the next.

Business cards and stationery

Business cards are a very good and useful form of drawing attention to your business. There are circumstances where you cannot really give out brochures to all and sundry but a business card with the name and nature of the business, the main contact details and even a picture of the property itself is a very effective marketing tool.

You can certainly produce these yourself but perhaps in this instance a professional job would be better. Keep some in the car and about your person, ready for use. We have given out cards on the most unlikely occasions – on a walk by the river where we met a dog owner interested in holiday cottage accommodation for the future and in a local shop where we overheard someone asking about self catering in the area.

Use headed notepaper designed for your business. Your stationery should feature the name of your establishment and the contact details. Do not be tempted to use too picturesque a typeface for this. In some cases this makes the wording very hard to read, which rather defeats the purpose of the exercise. If you want also to feature a small picture, remember that this will use a lot of different coloured inks when you are sending out letters every day, and may not really add anything useful to the letter.

You can do the complete layout on the computer when writing the letter – or print the letter text onto pre-printed, headed paper.

Tourist Boards

Joining a Tourist Board means that you can then use them in marketing your property. This is not just advertising in the different brochures they produce but taking advantage of the various marketing campaigns they run. Send for details to the individual Tourist Boards or check their websites. Every year new campaigns for seasonal holidays, outdoor activity holidays, golfing holidays etc are launched. There are also promotions round Britain and abroad at which you can have your brochures distributed. The Tourist Boards also have themed displays on occasion, at exhibitions and visitor centres, where they will display your information.

The brochures themselves offer a wide range of advertising and, with judicial selection, you can pick the most effective for you. Contact the Tourist Board to receive information concerning all the different forms of advertising you can participate in. Advertising this way can be expensive so you must make sure the cost is worth it. Having said this, it is difficult to tell until the end of the first year whether your advertisement has paid off.

Each Tourist Board also has its own website featuring an accommodation section where, in some cases, bookings can be taken online. You can choose which weeks you would like to have advertised with online booking (check the charge) and this is a useful additional facility to your normal booking procedure. Have a look at the relevant website and see how similar properties are depicted.

Tourist Boards reach a wide range of potential visitors, particularly those from abroad, and are often the first port of call for those coming to Britain.

Advertising text

For both the brochures and the website, choose your wording with care. Check the advertisements for similar properties. What is it about them that is attractive? You will only be allowed so many words – make them effective. Why should the visitor pick your property rather than any other? First impressions count and on a webpage you will probably have no second chance as there are so many alternative properties out there. What makes yours unique? This is where your marketing plan can help. What sort of holidaymakers are you trying to reach and what special features does your property have that makes it ideal for them? It may be no more complicated than being within walking distance of the centre of a historic town or close to Alton Towers. Whatever it is, do not forget to mention it. Of course you need also to have details of the accommodation itself – not too much, as there will be symbols with the text to show the individual facilities.

Check points

There are a number of important points to remember here.

+ Deciding on your marketing strategy and drawing up a plan for the way forward are essential for good and effective marketing of your property.

+ There are holiday cottage agencies which will market your property for you, answer enquiries and take bookings – but you will pay for this.

Commission is usually charged at a rate of approximately 20%, though this varies.

◆ Think laterally in order to reach the market you want for your properties.

◆ It is essential to have your own website, designed either by yourself or by a professional website designer. This should include all the details of your cottages, pictures, efficient links between pages, weekly prices with terms and conditions of booking and directions to your cottages.

◆ Advertising on commercial sites is necessary. Choose ones dedicated to self catering or for the niche market you are hoping to attract.

◆ Newspapers provide a useful last minute source of advertising, particularly for available weeks that are hard to book. Make sure you include details of your establishment with the address and all the other contact details, as well as any particular features you think would attract the visitor.

◆ Magazine advertising can be very effective, particularly in the niche market you are aiming for. More general magazines are also useful but often quite expensive.

◆ Your own brochure is an essential advertising tool. You can create this yourself or use a printing company. Creating your own enables you to amend details with ease and is more economical but the professional job usually looks better.

◆ You will need your own business cards and headed stationery. The cards, being easily carried, are useful for handing out at informal meetings and gatherings. You can create letters with suitable headings from the computer when required.

◆ The National Tourist Boards provide a good source for advertising as they can reach a wide audience including the foreign visitor, but they are very expensive. Choose which brochure you wish to advertise in with care.

PROGRESS PLAN

1. Draw up a marketing strategy for the sorts of visitors you hope to attract, list all the possible media for advertising you would use.

_____

_____

2. Investigate possibilities for your own website. Note down all the details that you would want to include. Explore the costs involved in having a website designed professionally.

_____

_____

3. Start to draw up a design for your own brochure. If you have a suitable package on your computer, either use one of the wizards available or design a brochure from scratch. What information would you include?

_____

_____

In conclusion

The marketing and advertising of your holiday business is of the utmost importance. It is how you present your services to the customer – how you want to be thought of in their eyes. Getting it right will lead to success for your venture.

Assuming now that you have reached the point where your marketing strategy is clearly thought out and your advertising arranged, you cannot sit back and relax. You still need to review the situation frequently. Advertisers will be contacting you all the time and you may need to rethink some of your publicity material if one advertisment does not seem to be working effectively.

Keep an open mind. If good opportunities arise, then consider them. On the other hand, you should be working to a budget so do not be tempted to take up every offer. Work out which you think will be most effective and maintain a watching brief. Develop a hard skin in order to say 'no' convincingly, as you will be contacted by many prospective advertisers as your business becomes better known.

14

Running the Business

You now have a proper marketing strategy, having chosen your target customers, worked out how to reach them and, of course, how to attract them to your property. You know what you intend to provide in the way of facilities and you are confident that your accommodation is exactly what the visitor is looking for on their holiday.

The stage is set. Are you now ready for that first enquiry from a prospective holidaymaker? Will you know how to deal with it and how to carry the enquiry through to an actual booking?

First, however, you will need to consider drawing up a **booking form** and a set of **terms and conditions** for the letting properties. Many small self catering businesses exist quite happily without either of these – indeed we have never issued booking forms ourselves but simply ask the visitor to send a letter with details of their booking along with their deposit. We have only three properties however. If you have a high number of cottages, then providing a booking form makes sense. The decision is yours.

The booking form

If you do issue a booking form it should include the following details for the visitor to complete:

◆ name and address;

◆ telephone number;

◆ email address;

◆ property to be booked;

◆ number in party (some businesses ask for names too);

◆ dates of booking period;

◆ amount to be paid as deposit (usually about one-fifth to one-third of the total cost of the holiday) or total amount if the holiday is imminent.

The booking form should be sent out to the prospective visitor when you receive an enquiry. It could also be included on your website for printing off by the prospective guest. You might also consider having a version you could send out by email – useful for visitors from abroad.

Terms and conditions

Many holiday businesses have a detailed sheet of terms and conditions which is sent with the booking form and also posted on their website. When a customer pays the initial deposit they are agreeing to abide by the terms and conditions set. It is of course up to you what you wish to include but you might consider some of the following:

◆ The time after which your visitor may arrive at the property at the beginning of their visit and the time they must leave by on the last day, e.g. 15.30 hours on the first day to 10.30 hours on the last.

◆ Any arrangements for dogs or other pets. If you charge for dogs, give the amount.

◆ Any extra charges for providing facilities for small children such as cots, high chairs, stair gates, etc.

◆ Any extras that will need to be paid for such as electricity, gas, heating, etc.

◆ Arrangements for payments e.g. bookings require a deposit of 30% at time of booking and the balance six weeks prior to arrival. In the case of a booking being made within the six weeks, the whole sum would be payable on booking.

◆ That the property should be left in a clean and decent condition. All breakages will be charged for. Give notice here, if you wish, that if extra cleaning is required over and above the normal you will charge a set sum for this. About £20 is reasonable.

◆ Number of guests. If you wish, make it clear that only the stipulated number of people can stay in any property. No surprise extra guests unless previously agreed.

◆ Cancellation (by guests) arrangements. These are important and should be very clear to all parties. You have several options. You can stipulate something along the lines of deposits are non-refundable and cancellation charges are 40% of balance if within four weeks of start date of holiday, 60% if within three weeks and 80% if within two weeks or less. Or you can offer to refund the deposit if you manage to re-book the period. It is possible too that if the stage has been reached where the balance has been paid over, you might retain all of this, suggesting that the visitor might consider taking out holiday insurance against this eventuality.

◆ Responsibility for possessions. Give notice that no responsibility can be accepted for personal possessions in the properties and for cars parked outside the properties.

♦ Cancellation (by you). State what will happen if for any reason you are unable to provide the property as booked. Perhaps you could agree to provide alternative accommodation in another of your properties or somewhere close by. If this is not possible then you should refund, in full, the cost of the holiday.

Before even the first enquiry comes through you should set up any pro forma letters you will need for enquiries, and for acknowledgements of deposits, balances and total amounts. These can be kept fairly simple but in all cases it is a nice touch to include the name of the recipient – not entered afterwards by hand but as part of the printed letter.

Pro forma letters

Draw up a basic letter on your word processor which you can adapt if necessary to answer specific enquiries or to add a personal note if the visitor is a regular one. You will need the following:

♦ **Letter re enquiry**. This letter would accompany a brochure or brochures and need only include thanks for the enquiry and answers to any queries made, including that of availability.

♦ **Acknowledgement of deposit**. Include thanks for the payment, the amount, the cottage booked, the dates and confirmation of any agreed extra facilities such as cot or high chair. It should also give details of the balance and when it is due. You might include details of any insurance company dealing with holiday insurance that your visitor could contact directly.

♦ **Acknowledgement of balance**. Again include the amount of the payment with thanks, the dates and cottage booked and time of entry to the property. You should also give any information you think necessary for the holidaymaker to know in advance i.e. directions to the property, and locations and times of opening of local shops if the cottage is in fairly remote territory.

♦ **Acknowledgement of total amount**. Sometimes the visitor will book the holiday at the last moment and will be sending the full amount on booking. In this case the letter will follow much the same lines as the acknowledgement of the balance.

Enquiries and bookings

Now you are fully prepared for the first communication from your prospective visitor. Are you ready to take a booking – or, perhaps initially, to answer an enquiry?

Answering an enquiry

Unless you are already established as a holiday cottage business, your first communication will probably be an enquiry. This may be for a brochure only or might be the first step towards an actual booking. Nowadays this enquiry will take the form of a telephone call, email and, on the extremely rare occasion, a letter. Even though you are fully booked for the period of time the visitor is interested in, you should always answer the enquiry as fully as possible, even when this is a telephone message or is sent by email. If you cannot accommodate them this time they may call back again for a booking for their next holiday. Can you suggest somewhere else they could try on this occasion? Perhaps you may risk losing them altogether if they like the other cottage, but on the other hand you will hopefully impress them with how busy (with all your cottages fully booked) and how helpful you are.

Telephone call

This can come at any time and you must be ready for it. It may seem obvious but remember to have paper and pens close to your telephone. If you have telephones in different rooms the same applies to every one of them. The caller may have seen your advertisement in a publication, spotted your website or might have heard of your cottages from someone else. They may know a great deal about the facilities available or practically nothing at all. It will be up to you to turn this enquiry into a firm booking if possible.

Find out the size of the party, which cottage they are interested in (if they have already made up their mind) and the dates of their holiday. They may require information from you about whether the property is available, the facilities it has, the surrounding area, the access and many other points.

If all they are immediately interested in is a brochure you will need a name and address with postcode. Make sure you get the spelling correct. Note the information and record it somewhere along with any other contact details you have (phone number, email address, etc). You might consider a book or file to hold enquiries with dates though this could get very unwieldy over the following months. Promise to send a brochure immediately and do so. If they mention a date for their holiday, enquire if they would like you to make a provisional booking for them and tell them for how long you will hold this booking.

Ask if they have access to the web and, if they do, point them in the direction of your website where they will find most of the information they will need. This does not mean you should not be sending a brochure, though, as many people like to see the printed word in front of them and perhaps send it on to their family or friends.

If the enquiry comes as a message on your answer machine reply to it as soon as possible.

◆ **TOP TIP** ◆

Ask where the caller heard about your property – it will help you find out which advertising is the most effective for your business.

Email

This is an increasingly popular way of enquiring about accommodation. It is easy and quick but can be rather impersonal. Check your email regularly and acknowledge all messages as soon as possible. With this method of enquiry the request can still be for a brochure, but is more likely to be about availability. If the request is for a brochure, again point the enquirer in the direction of your website – they may not have realised you have one – but also send the brochure.

In your email reply be informative, courteous and expand a little on the original enquiry. For instance, if they say they have small children offer a cot or high chair (if you provide them) and mention any particular facilities or attractions for children in the area. In other words – show willing.

Even though email is a very informal means of communication, make sure that all your messages are professional. This does not mean that they have to be strictly formal – this would be rather ridiculous – but there should be no typing errors, no spelling mistakes and the message should not be in a style of writing that is abbreviated and/or hard to understand.

There may be something in the email to indicate where the enquirer got your email address from, as some of the cottage websites have enquiry forms with their name included. If not, again try to find out. It is useful research for you to see which of your advertisements or website entries are working.

Letter
An enquiry by letter is very rare but it can happen. With this form of communication you will have the name, address and perhaps the telephone number also. Send off the brochure straight away, including any details they have asked for. If there is a telephone number, it might be a good idea to ring them and ask if they have any specific dates in mind.

Taking a booking

Taking a booking is the next stage in the procedure, though sometimes it can be combined with the enquiry. This is the point you have been working towards and waiting for. How are you going to record these bookings? If you have a few cottages only, then a large book is sufficient or, if you prefer, bookings can be recorded on your computer. In either case the method is the same. Divide the left hand column into weeks with prices and head a column with the name of each property.

Once you have a firm booking, enter it in the appropriate space with name, telephone number and any other details you will need to hand, such as any extras to be provided. If the party is leaving earlier than the usual Saturday leaving date, then record the date of departure. If they are bringing a dog or need a high chair, enter this too. Once a deposit has been paid, record this with the date and the amount. The same applies for the balance.

The advantage of using a book is that it can always be to hand when you get a telephone call. You can easily check if the week is available and record the booking quickly. Those who prefer to use a computer will argue that the information is easier to read (this depends on your handwriting) and can be updated very simply. The only problem is that you might write down the information on paper in the interim but forget to update your computer booking list. Trying to get into the computer in a hurry while your guest is waiting on the phone can be difficult sometimes as the phone call can come at any time, day or evening.

If you have a higher number of properties, the time-honoured wall board is excellent. It is immediately obvious whether a week is booked or whether it is available. The necessary information can then be added to the board. You might also keep a back-up system going on the computer.

However you choose to use to record them, you must be ready for bookings to come in by telephone, email and letter.

- **Telephone.** If someone phones you to make a booking then you have the option of either sending them the booking form to be returned with the deposit or of asking them to send you a letter with the deposit and details of the holiday they wish to book. Record the booking at the time and once the booking form or letter arrives, send a letter of confirmation immediately. They will want confirmation that you have received their payment – so do not delay replying to them. File the letter or booking form for future reference.

  The party may wish to pay by credit card. In this case you will need a name and address to send the letter of confirmation with a copy of the card transaction.

- **Email.** Often when a booking arrives by email, the payment follows by post. Acknowledge the booking immediately by return email, record it in the book as a probable booking and wait for the arrival of the cheque. Once the payment has come, send a letter of confirmation as above. If you wish to send a booking form to be completed by the party, explain this in the email.

◆ **Online booking.** This is increasingly used in the accommodation
sector but booking a self catering holiday is not the same as booking a
hotel or B&B. Most visitors want to talk to you, the owner, before
booking. There are always details to discuss and visitors like to get an
idea of the finer points of the accommodation (and owners!) they are
coming to.

I think that many self caterers would agree that this works both ways.
We like to get an idea of our visitor too. It is at this stage that you can
tactfully filter out those guests who might not be totally acceptable to
you or who might find the sort of holiday you are providing is wrong for
them – and make this plain on arrival at your property! In the end it is
your property and your responsibility. You might want to exclude stag
or hen parties, for example, or want to warn large parties coming at
Christmas or New Year that you do not accept extra guests in sleeping
bags. You might live in a remote area and want to check with your
visitor that they realise exactly how far the nearest shop or pub is and
how long it takes to reach your property from the city, for example.

◆ **TOP TIP** ◆

It is good to establish some form of real communication with your guest
before they arrive – both for your benefit and for theirs. We have many
regular visitors and they always like a chat by phone or email before
booking. I do not think many of them would take kindly to the impersonal
nature of online booking alone.

Methods of payment

We have had payments made by cash, cheque, international money
transfer, postal order and credit or debit card. Payments by cash are
unusual but they do happen. This tends to be when the booking is at
such short notice that there is no time to send a cheque. If this is the
case, insist on cash on arrival, to get the financial transaction out of the
way. Avoid, if you can, making large payments of cash into your business
account as you will be charged for it. In fact you will find that using a
business account in many banks is expensive. You will be charged for

any transaction across the counter, for the cheque or cash you pay in, for any cheques you pay out and for direct debits on the account. You might consider, if you are a small business, using a separate personal account for your business unless you can find a bank that has a reasonable attitude towards small businesses.

Payments made by international money transfer are expensive for the guest who will have to absorb the cost of the transfer. They will also need your bank details for their own bank to carry out the transfer. For these reasons, this is not an ideal method of payment.

More and more people want to make payments by credit or debit cards. It is quick and easy for them and has advantages for you too. The payments can be made at the time of booking over the telephone and you do not have to wait for the cheque. A card payment also takes less time to clear than a cheque. Credit cards are thus another good method of payment for those last minute bookings.

Enquire at your bank about renting an electronic terminal. You may have to pay a one-off registration fee. You will have to pay a monthly rental, of course, and a fee, depending on the type of card, for every transaction. Will the benefits outweigh the cost? This is dependent on how much you use the facility and is very hard to assess in advance but part of your decision should be the ease of booking using card transactions. If you do sign up to it, you will have to hire the terminal for a given period of time, possibly a minimum of three years, so be sure that you know all the details of costs involved before you start. If you decide to cancel the arrangement within this time frame, you will incur a charge.

When you take a booking by card, it is best to have the numbers read out over the telephone. Most people realise that an email is not secure but we have had credit card numbers sent in this way. Make sure to discourage this if it is suggested by the visitor.

If you do decide to rent a terminal the bank will ask you to open a business account (if you do not have one already) for the purpose.

There is the other option of having an online booking service with a secure site for payments. You can purchase software for this purpose. If you buy into this, make sure that the site you use is easily operated and secure – and recommended by other businesses if possible.

Insurance

There are two kinds of insurance that you will reqire. For the purposes of letting holiday cottages you will need to take out insurance for the business and then there is the question of cancellation insurance for the holiday.

There are certain insurance companies (see Appendix) which specialise in insuring holiday cottages. These will provide you with cover for:

♦ buildings and trade contents;

♦ public liability;

♦ employers' liability for any employees you have;

♦ cover for loss of rental income and cost of alternative accommodation following loss or damage to the property.

Cancellation of a holiday can cause a lot of ill feeling if not handled carefully. It is up to you to decide how to deal with this. There needs to be a statement in the terms and conditions that will set matters out clearly to the visitor. If you do not issue a document with terms and conditions, then you should make clear on your website and in your brochure what is expected of your visitor.

You have two real options open to you. You can bear the cost of cancellation yourself (possibly deducting a charge for administration from the deposit) or you can offer your visitors a cancellation insurance scheme by sending them forms in order that they can deal with the company direct. This is no guarantee, of course, that they will take out the insurance. You may be able to re-let the week easily and in any case cancellation does not occur very often in our experience. If you do decide to send out forms for the visitors to choose whether to take out insurance, you cannot legally benefit from any commission from the insurance company, without being formally registered as an agent.

Any other possibilities, such as running your own insurance scheme (illegal now unless you are prepared to become an accredited agency by passing various examinations) or insisting that visitors pay for cancellation insurance by charging for it as a condition of booking, become very complex. If you are interested in either of these possibilities you should take legal advice.

Although we have a cancellation policy in force we very rarely enforce it, preferring to take each case on its own merits. Most people do not cancel their holiday on a whim. In all our cases to date, cancellation has been due to a visitor's discovery of a medical condition and has been totally unavoidable. You do want the visitor to feel able to come back to your property another time – and this is the whole point – you want to resolve the situation to the satisfaction of both of you. Try to be flexible.

Keeping guest records

So what kind of records do you need to keep in relation to your guests? You should certainly keep records of all communications between you and them but how much more do you need?

- Booking forms and/or letters with booking requests with name, address, telephone number and (possibly) the email address of the person booking the holiday.

- Any emails with booking instructions. Again this should include the full name and address of the person concerned.

- A record of when you replied to each booking request – this can be as straightforward as writing 'replied 2 Aug 2004' on the booking form, letter or email copy.

- Note of all payments – deposits, balances, total amounts and the date when paid.

- Note of the payee's name on the paying in book slip.

♦ Note of any extra requirements you have agreed to provide.

♦ Bank statements showing payments made into the account(s).

♦ Copies of the credit card/debit card transactions. Attach these to the relevant letter, booking form or email for safekeeping in your records.

♦ Complete record of your property 'weeks' with dates booked, name of guest responsible for party, deposits and balances paid with dates of payment.

You might also like to keep a written list of 'regulars' to refer to. Why not offer them a discount, send them a Christmas card, provide them with a bottle of wine when they arrive or write acquainting them of any special offers or events? Consider this as part of your marketing strategy. In fact, once they have become well established return visitors, we tend to send them a hand written confirmation of their booking rather than the standard letter.

Simple book-keeping

Good book-keeping is essential to your business. Start as you mean to go on and try to keep everything up to date – it is all too easy to lose receipts and forget transactions. We started with a very simple paper-based system and it has stood us in good stead. If you prefer to use a computer-based system there are several excellent software packages you can buy (see Appendix).

Keeping records
What records do you need? You need to record all the money coming into your business and going out. This is for tax purposes but also for your own benefit – you have to keep track of income and expenditure. Number and date all your invoices or receipts and file them in date order. Be rigorous about marking cheque stubs with the amount, date and what the cheque was for. You will need to keep:

♦ Receipts for all purchases you make in connection with the business – for furniture, fuel, bedding, curtains, lamps, white goods, etc.

- Receipts for petrol you used when travelling on business. It is sometimes difficult to assess the exact amount spent on business travel when you go to the shops for example, so we make over a certain percentage of the fuel bill for our self catering business.

- Invoices for work carried out on the properties.

- Records of any cash payment you made or was made to you – receipt or a written record.

- Bank statements from your business account(s).

- Records of any mortgage or loan repayments.

- Records of any payments made to you by the visitors – deposits and receipts. When paying these into the bank, mark the stub of the paying in slip with the amount, date or invoice number and the name of the visitor.

The cash book

You will need to note all this information either on your software package or in a cash book – with several columns on each page. Our business is not very complex and we do not expect it to become so. We have successfully used this paper system for all the years we have been trading.

In the front part of the book we have a double page for each month. Starting from the left, the columns are headed with date, item of purchase or expenditure, receipt number, the amount as a cheque (with cheque number) or cash, and then the different categories of expenditure. You will have your own ideas on these but some of the more obvious ones might be advertising, travel, postage, building work, furniture, contents, capital items, running costs such as electricity and telephone, decoration, DIY and office materials. Ask your accountant if you are not sure of the categories to use. The last column we head 'drawings'. This holds the amounts we take out of the business. In the column for item of expenditure we note where the money goes – to our personal account perhaps. This is so that we can keep track of it.

Each item is entered in date order (if possible). Looking at a typical month we have a wide range of purchases and expenditure such as cot sheets, a book on web page design, bedding, petrol, two magazine advertisements, a subscription to a self catering organisation, a plumbing bill, insurance for the properties and a new clothes dryer for one of the cottages.

The amount for each of these items is entered twice – once under cheque or cash and once under the appropriate heading. For certain payments such as petrol, telephone, oil and electricity we enter a fixed percentage only of the amount (approved by our accountant). The Inland Revenue also need to be convinced, of course!

A very simple example of a page of items of expenditure would look like the one in Figure 2.

April									
Date	Item	Rec no.	Cheque no	Cheque	Cash	Advert-ising	Contents	Postage	Drawings
6	Cot sheets	72			7.99		7.99		
8	Stamps	73			5.40			5.40	
17	To personal account			200.00					200.00
20	Advert	74	111111	72.00		72.00			
30	2 lamps	75	111112	35.00			35.00		
	Total			307.00	13.39	72.00	42.99	5.40	200.00

Fig. 2. Cash book: Expenditure.

At the end of the month all the columns are totalled and the figures checked for accuracy. The total of the two columns for cheque and cash should add up to the total of all the other columns.

At the back of the book we record all the income we receive and where it comes from (see Figure 3). For income from the property we note the name of the visitor, whether they are paying the deposit, balance or total amount and the dates they have booked. It makes it much easier when trying to tie up amounts in this book with bank statements later. We also note which property they have booked, using the initial letter of the name of the cottage, S, K or G.

January							
Date	Source	Property	Banked	Credit card	Cash	Cottage income	Workshops
4	Mackenzie, tot, Jan 3–10	S	180.00			180.00	
6	Holmes, dep, Jun 22–Jul 6	K	264.00			264.00	
23	Smart, bal, Mar 23–30	G	210.00			210.00	
30	Ashley, tot, Feb 23–Mar 2	S		195.00		195.00	
30	Britten, tot, Jan 30–Feb 1	S			60.00	60.00	
31	Basket making				250.00		250.00
	Total		654.00	195.00	310.00	909.00	250.00

Figure 3. Cash book: income.

At the end of the month the total of the three columns headed 'banked', 'cash' and 'credit card' should add up to the same total as the rest of the columns.

Check points

♦ To summarise the important points in this chapter:

♦ Part of running the business successfully involves carrying out the many administrative tasks, such as taking bookings, answering enquiries, dealing with payments, etc, correctly and on time.

♦ The booking form, to be completed by your prospective visitors, should include the details of name and address, telephone number, email address, property name, number in party and dates of the booking period along with the sum to be paid.

♦ It is advised that a detailed list of terms and conditions should be issued to the visitor and agreed by them. This should include:
  – Days and times of arrival and departure.
  – Arrangements for any pets.

- Arrangements for any small children such as cost of hiring cots, etc.
- Extras to be paid for.
- Payment arrangements for deposits, etc.
- Statement that property to be left in a clean and decent condition, all breakages to be paid for and notice of any deposit for this.
- Your charges/arrangements if the guest cancels.
- Arrangements for any occasion when you are unable to provide the booked accommodation.
- Notice of no responsibility accepted by you for guests possessions, cars, etc.

♦ It is useful to have a set of pro forma letters drawn up, to be sent by you in confirmation of any payments made or with a brochure when there is an enquiry. These can be adapted when necessary for a more personal approach.

♦ You should be prepared to answer the telephone calls at any time with courtesy and a professional approach. The same applies to email messages, which should be well set out, free of spelling errors and clearly understandable to the recipient.

♦ All messages, either left on the answering machine or by email or letter, should be answered as soon as possible. Any brochures requested should also be sent straight away, as should confirmations of bookings and payments.

♦ Record any bookings immediately, either in a book, on a wall board or perhaps by computer. You should note names and any extras to be provided. Keep an accurate check on all payments made.

♦ Payments can be made by cheque, postal order, cash, international money transfer and by credit or debit card. It may be worth renting an electronic terminal though you will have to pay a monthly rental, a fee for every transaction and possibly a one-off registration fee.

♦ Online booking is becoming increasingly popular generally in the tourist industry, though the use of this facility without any customer contact is not popular with many self caterers and their visitors, who prefer some form of communication first.

♦ As a self catering business owner, you must take out insurance for your business to cover the buildings and contents themselves, public liability, employers' liability for any employees and cover for loss of rental due to damage to the property. You can also give your guests notice of an insurance scheme in case of cancellation.

♦ You should keep all guest records of:
  – booking forms;
  – communications with the guest;
  – payments with amount, name of guest, date of holiday and payment;
  – extra requirements you will provide;
  – bank statements showing payments into your business account;
  – credit card slips;
  – all bookings;
  – paying in slips.

♦ Good book-keeping is necessary to achieve business success. All transactions should be noted, receipts and invoices filed as well as records of any payments both by you (purchases, advertisements, etc) and to you (bookings, grants, interest amounts, etc) kept.

♦ The cash book is a simple concept but this, or a slightly more complex software package, will allow you to note all expenditure and payments. If you think that your business is going to get more complex, start off with the software package.

PROGRESS PLAN

There is a great deal to digest in this chapter but it will all become second nature to you very quickly.

1. Draw up a booking form for your business and a list of terms and conditions that will apply to the visitor.

----

2. Investigate the possibility of renting an electronic terminal and find out the actual costs involved.

----

3. Either draw up a cash book for the business with all the headings for purchases you will need or investigate software packages for carrying out this function on the computer.

----

4. Prepare a wall board, bookings book or computer file or spreadsheet to record all your bookings and payments for the cottages for a year ahead.

After the booking

You are now confident about dealing with enquiries about your holiday properties. You know how you will record bookings with deposits and balance payments. You are hopefully becoming flexible about methods of payment and know about the records necessary for the smooth running of the business. So far you have communicated with your guests by phone, letter or email. Now you are going to have to deal with the guest in person. Are you confident about this?

15

Providing the Service

Of course you want to make your business a success and a large part of this success will be due to the way you treat your guests. Will you greet them personally when they arrive at their holiday cottage? Think about what your attitude will be when they ask for help or information and just how friendly you have to be. A holiday cottage is not the same as a B&B – you will not have guests in the house and in some instances you might hardly see them at all. This makes it all the more important to make the right impression when you do see them. And just how much in the way of extras are you willing to provide, or will you stick strictly to the terms of your letting agreement?

You want your guests to return, of course, but it is not just that. You are in the business of providing holidays for people and what better business could you be in than one which provides relaxation, enjoyment and pleasure? Yes, there will always be the difficult guests or the truly demanding, but there are so many people who will really appreciate the atmosphere of a cottage that is comfortable, warm and inviting. We see visitors arriving stressed and tense from a busy schedule at work, who after a few days in the cottages change completely. We often find them standing smiling, quietly admiring the scenery or watching the birdlife!

Attitude

Your attitude to any interaction with your guest or prospective guest is of prime importance. You will have been in contact with them on the telephone, by email or letter, and when they arrive at the property you will be talking to them during their stay and, of course, saying goodbye when they leave.

Telephone, email, letter

We have covered the subject of enquiries and bookings in a previous chapter but it is important to emphasise that your attitude on the phone will make a real difference. Even if the call has come at an inconvenient time you should try to put a smile in your voice. If they are asking for information, take time to answer, do not just give them bare facts. They might want to discuss the difference between cottages or ask for the cost of a short break. They cannot possibly know that you were just sitting down to eat or on the way out to the shops. And even if they did, this is a business you are running and you should always try to take a professional approach.

Returning an email message is easier in some ways. You can consider your answer more carefully, but it is still important to reply as soon as you can and to give as much information as possible to help the visitor. Your attitude will be apparent through the words you use. Thank them for their message and supply them with what they need in the way of information or help. Suggest other possibilities, if you cannot accommodate them. Make your cottages sound inviting by mentioning any special features such as real fires in the winter months, views of the countryside or perhaps even all-inclusive pricing, cutting out those extra costs. If they like the sound of you and your properties they may contact you another time.

It may be that it is not you or your partner who answers the phone, but one of your family. Make sure they know how to respond to prospective visitors and how to deal with enquiries. If they are willing to help, there is no reason why they should not be as pleasant and efficient as you at taking calls but if they are unwilling, at least persuade them to take a proper message with the name and phone number of the caller. Then answer the call yourself as soon as possible.

Your letters should be clear and informative but not too impersonal. If you are replying to someone who has visited the cottages before you might like to add some personal note. Again your attitude in letters should be friendly but professional.

Greeting guests

A great deal depends on whether you live on site or not. If you live at some distance and employ someone to clean and look after the cottages, or even if you clean the cottages yourself but still live some distance away, then a face to face encounter may be less likely. However, running it as a larger business, many of you will be living close to your holiday homes. If you are, aim to be there in person when the guests arrive. You can always give them a time slot – between 3.30pm and 6.30pm perhaps – with the proviso that if they are going to be later than this they should phone to warn you.

If you have a small number of cottages you can probably identify the guests as they arrive, but if you are running a larger business you will have to wait until they identify themselves. Check the names of the arriving guests in advance so you know how many and who to expect. If you remember them from a previous visit, well and good – people like to be recognised.

You will want to give them a brief tour of the cottage, answering any particular queries and emphasising any important points. Do not provide a barrage of information though – they have probably travelled a long way and all they want to do is unload the luggage, get settled in and make a cup of tea. Greet them politely, be friendly and then leave them alone. With most of your guests, this is sufficient for the day. What sometimes happens is that five minutes later there will be a knock at the door and someone will be standing there with a question. They may not know how to work the television controls, they may have forgotten to bring towels or they want to know if the nearby shop will still be open. Hopefully you will not be dealing with a complaint, especially at this early stage. Be pleasant to them, even if you have told them the same thing just a few minutes ago.

During the holiday

If you live close by or on site you will probably see quite a lot of your guests during the week. How friendly should you be? Visitors vary widely. There are some who prefer to spend the holiday strictly on their own without talking or communicating with you or the other guests and this is their privilege. They usually have all their trips well thought out in advance and do not need to ask for advice. A friendly wave or word in passing is all they want and it is easy to provide this. Other visitors want a more interactive approach. They like to stop for a chat when they see you. They may want to talk about the area or ask about places to visit. It might not always be convenient but try to accommodate them. In smaller communities, it is quite likely that you may meet your guests in passing in the local shop, at an event, or whatever. They will expect to be recognised, even for a passing greeting – keep an eye open for them. It is this friendly attitude that means so much to them. It helps to make them feel at home and relaxed on their holiday. It may also make them want to return for another visit.

If they have a dog, they may want to find places for walks. Presumably you only allow dogs in your properties if you like them, so it is not a hardship to be friendly to the dog as well as to the owner.

◆ **TOP TIP** ◆

> Respond to the guest as an individual. If they seem to prefer being alone, leave them in peace without taking offence or trying to engage them in conversation. If they are friendly, respond in the same vein.

It is a good idea to try to talk to your guest on the day after they arrive to enquire if there are any problems or if there is any piece of equipment they cannot find in the cottage. It is as well to hear about this near the start of the holiday when you can do something about it. Remember this may be their one week of holiday away from home for the whole year – it has got to be a special, enjoyable experience for them.

At the end

The last day of the holiday has arrived and your guest is packing up. Do not hang around waiting for them to leave or engage them in a long conversation when they are trying to pack the car. Usually, if you are on site, your visitors will ring the doorbell to tell you they are leaving and to hand in the key. Again, if they are in a hurry be pleasant and wish them safe journey. Do not pressurise them by asking if they will be back the following year. If *they* stop for a chat or mention returning the next year, then all well and good.

It is at this point that they may tell you about any breakages they have had or any problems. It can be annoying to hear that they have not found some particular piece of equipment that you know is in the cottage or have not been able to work the shower, for example. Be polite, show concern, and assure them that you will look into it at once. If it is something that might have repercussions, you might decide to look into it in their presence, if you are fairly sure that there is a solution.

Remember that you want them to leave their holiday home with happy memories.

What to provide

In providing an excellent service for your guests you might want to go that little bit further to make their holiday a special one. Your properties have all the facilities, comfort and cleanliness that you have promised in your brochure and on the website but there might be some extras which you could consider that would raise the standard of your accommodation from good to memorable.

Welcome pack

It is a nice touch to put in a few groceries to welcome your visitors. This can be as simple as tea, coffee, sugar and milk. Some other items you might consider are bread (especially if you bake your own), a bottle of wine, biscuits, eggs or a cake. If you like, use your imagination and find something interesting, local and unusual to leave for them.

Perhaps you might think of providing a shopping service, getting in groceries in advance for your guests, to be paid for when they arrive. This would save them carrying large amounts of food with them as well as all their luggage. Of course this is not always possible as many holiday cottages are far from supermarkets or even from small grocery shops and you would have to shop for everything well in advance.

Extras

Bed linen and towels are often expected as part of the holiday package. At least if you provide the bed linen you can make the rooms look good when the visitors arrive and it saves problems with duvet sizes, blankets, etc. You should provide new toilet rolls in all the bathrooms too, of course. Over and above the facilities and equipment you would expect to find in a holiday property, you might also consider providing bath mats, tea towels, kitchen towel, some washing tablets and dish washer tablets, if there is a dishwasher. Most of these are small items but are very much appreciated by the guest who has probably forgotten to bring some of them.

It is important not to get carried away with providing extras for the visitors. You have to consider the financial side of things, but many of these suggestions do not cost very much. However, if you do find that it is too expensive or time consuming, then cut back a little and simply put in only what you consider worthwhile.

If you have an open fire or stove in the property, do you provide coal or logs for it? It is a nice touch to have the fire set and some logs and coal beside it for the first evening. You could always have coal available for purchase as an extra. In the depth of winter if we know the time of arrival of our visitors we try to have the fire lit in advance. It makes for a very warm welcome, literally.

On the second or third day, check that they have managed to get the fire going again. As mentioned before, some people have had little experience of open fires.

Then there are the special occasions. If you have honeymooners booked in or couples coming to celebrate an anniversary, why not provide a bottle of wine or even champagne and a card? If they are honeymooners, they may come back again for their first or subsequent anniversary. Perhaps a child from one of the families holidaying in your properties will have a birthday while they are there. Would you consider giving them a card and/or a small present?

At Christmas would you consider providing a tree with lights? The visitors, if advised, could bring their own decorations. It is a special time of year and more and more people are taking a break away at this season.

Information

You will have all the official tourist information in the properties as a matter of course. It is also a good idea to provide leaflets for attractions, events, walks, festivals, parks, etc in the immediate area and within easy travelling distance. Be sure to update these every year – entrance charges and costs will vary from year to year and out of date information can be irritating – especially if the attraction has closed down in the interim.

What about drawing up your own set of informal guides to car journeys and walks in the area? This is a pleasant winter task and makes the information that bit more personalised. There are often special places that only people who live locally would know about or stories that are part of folklore in your area. Reading about these can make the visitor feel part of the local scene, which some of them love.

Then there is the strictly practical information you should provide – telephone numbers for the doctor, dentist, local police, coast guard or mountain rescue (if appropriate), hospital and garage. There should also be details of pubs, restaurants and hotels in the area as well as about useful shops such as a good butcher, delicatessen or baker. It is always difficult to recommend restaurants to people as tastes and pockets differ widely. Perhaps it is better to name them all (within reason) with any official recommendations that they have. If you live in an area where restaurants close relatively early in the evening, then it is only fair to warn your visitor, particularly if they are from Europe where they may be accustomed to eating quite late at night.

Assistance

Just how helpful are you prepared to be? If your visitor's car is stuck at the bottom of the drive in the snow, are you willing to tow them up to the house? If you live in a remote area, you might have to. If they have an accident, what will you do? It is your decision about how much you are going to put yourself out for your guests. It is certainly easier to help those who are pleasant to you. If you have an awkward visitor it is sometimes tempting to leave them to their own devices but this is not good policy. Anyone can be bad tempered in a situation where they feel stressed. Help them out of it and you are a friend!

Foreign visitors might need assistance with booking particular events or activities. If you are asked about golf or horse riding, for instance, can you find out the information for them and even go so far as to phone to book your guest in for a round or lesson? Those visitors from Europe and beyond might need more attention than guests from the UK, unless they have visited the country before.

If someone becomes ill in the night, do you know what to do? Keep up to date with the arrangements for how the local medical services respond to out of hours calls.

Then there are the bigger emergencies, usually taking place in the winter months – flooded roads, major accidents, trees down and transport problems. It is only considerate to warn your visitors in advance if they are due to arrive that day and the road is blocked for some reason. You might think that this sort of occurrence is rare but, listening to the weather forecasts, it appears that Britain is going to experience more extreme weather conditions in the future with higher rainfall and stronger winds. You would expect your visitor to check with the AA, for example, if there was some sort of emergency on the motorway, but they will not think to check about more local conditions. You can help them here.

What not to provide

It is just as important to consider what not to provide as to be aware of the positive.

Hidden extras

You should have made clear in your brochure and website any extras that your visitors will be expected to pay for such as electricity, towels, etc. It is very bad policy not to warn them of these in advance and may be contravening the Trade Descriptions Act. If they will need pound coins for a meter even, be sure to let them know before they arrive. There should be no unpleasant surprises for them when they come for their holiday.

Intrusiveness

It is possible to be too friendly towards your visitors. Most people will make plain just how much they want in the way of contact with you. It may sound obvious, but do not knock at the door of their cottage for a chat. If you are working outside in the garden, too, a friendly wave is enough as they pass you, unless they actually stop for a word. You do not want them to feel you are watching them.

Do not offer unwanted advice either. If they express an interest in going to some local attraction, it is fair to warn them about any particularly high costs involved perhaps, but do not offer a lengthy opinion on the merits of the attraction. You should be providing information on interesting days out, for example, but do not feel it necessary to give them a blow by blow account of everything they will see. People like to discover things for themselves and tastes differ widely. One person's fascinating day out at a castle is another's boring trip round some ruins.

If you have young children, let them know not to bother the visitors. Not everyone likes children or wants to talk to them – on their holiday particularly. It is usually fairly easy to gauge the feelings of the guests early on, however, and if they seem to be happy to talk to your children, that is fine. Keep an eye on them though so that you can tell when enough is enough. The same applies to animals. Keep your own in check and try to see to it that dogs belonging to the visitors do not annoy other guests.

Opinions

Your visitors will not want to hear your opinions of the political scene, the youth of today, religion, the police or any of the other topics you might feel strongly about. They may be to some extent a captive audience, but do not take advantage of this. They will probably be happy to pass the time of day with you or chat about this and that but do not inflict your beliefs, however strongly felt, on them.

They may, of course, inflict theirs on you. In this case you should deal with the situation politely and as briefly as possible without causing any offence.

Rules

Try not to have too many rules and regulations about the place. Notices can be off putting, especially when there are lots of them. If you have something to say about no smoking, the lighting of a stove or exactly what it is permissible to put down the loo, then try to keep any obvious instructions to a minimum and leave a sheet of important information about the cottage in a handy file.

The same applies to the garden and parking areas as to the inside of the properties. Discreet parking signs are fine but notices forbidding all sorts of activities create a hostile environment. If you allow animals in the cottages but need to restrict their activities outside, make sure the dog owners know where they can take them for a walk and of course you need to provide bins if you want to enforce a pooper scooper area round the buildings.

Entering properties

I would say that this is not something you should do unless invited in or it is really essential. The property is theirs for the period of their visit and an awareness that you have been wandering amongst their personal belongings while they were out will not make for a happy situation if they find out.

If you do need to gain entry for some work to be done or for a cottage inspection by a Quality Assurance inspector, for example, then ask your visitor if it would be okay before the event, and give them the opportunity of being there at the same time. Never leave any tradesmen or similar alone in the cottage with your visitor's possessions around, however official the visit may be.

Involvement

Make a real effort not to get involved in any quarrels or disagreements between visitors in the same group. If a visitor tries to take you aside to explain their side of an argument, resist politely. Be impartial and do not take sides. It will only cause ill-feeling and basically is nothing to do with you.

Disagreements between different groups of guests are trickier to deal with. After all they are on your property and you may feel that it is up to you to deal with the situation. If the argument is over something you do feel is your responsibility, then you should deal with it. For example, if one family's dog is annoying the children of another family then it may be up to you to approach the family with the dog and ask them to keep it under control. It may be, though, that the argument is strictly between guests. You do not want this to happen but it sometimes does and cannot be helped. If you can calm the situation down then fine, but try not to take sides or get drawn into the quarrel.

Questionnaires

Some holiday cottage owners like to issue questionnaires to the guests. These can provide a useful measure of how the visitor perceives your property and how your cottage compares with other similar ones.

There is no reason why you cannot draw up your own questionnaire but there are already various official versions which associations and tourist bodies can provide. If you can get hold of these they can give you a guide as to which questions you should be asking and how to set out the information. Or you can simply use them as they stand if you think they meet your purpose.

◆ **TOP TIP** ◆

Feedback from guests is one of the most useful ways of finding out about your accommodation.

The Quality Assurance inspection takes place on one day a year only and covers the properties from the Tourist Board's point of view. A visitor who has stayed in your property may notice entirely different things and, from their standpoint, may attach different levels of importance to those things. You can ask them for suggestions for improvement or make specific queries about features you have introduced or facilities you have included.

Some of the areas you might want to include in your questionnaire are:

◆ cleanliness;

◆ comfort;

◆ heating;

- lighting;

- furniture;

- equipment;

- facilities;

- quality of the services provided by owner, including directions, information, welcome, etc.

You can ask them to give these points a mark on a scale of 1 to 10.

You might ask them specific questions such as:

- How would they rate your property against others they have stayed in?

- Would they return to your property in the future?

- What suggestions would they make for improvements with regard to facilities or equipment?

Or you might have certain features in your cottages that you would like commented on. For instance, how important to the visitor are:

- ensuite bathrooms;

- open fires or stoves;

- traditional style cottages;

- a peaceful location;

- dogs made welcome;

- etc.

Certainly the answers you get will provide you with a very clear idea of the likes and dislikes of your guests. Similar answers from several guests will give you a clear indication of what the cottage is lacking or of where you are fulfilling all their needs. You may get some surprises too. Some guests may find the heating superb while others are very dissatisfied with it. Some will be happy with everything you have provided while others will list equipment they feel is missing. It is up to you to spot the recurring points and comments and work on those.

Open ended questions can sometimes be counterproductive however. Questions such as 'If we were to improve one item, what should it be?' can make the visitor struggle to come up with some sort of answer although they were really quite happy with everything in the cottage.

Sometimes you can pick up comments about faulty equipment (such as a leaking kettle or a 'dead' TV controller) that you probably would not notice at changeover. This potentially allows you to do something about it before the next guests arrive.

The questionnaire does not, however, replace the direct face to face contact during the visit. Simply asking your guest on day two whether everything is okay is much the best way of finding out if they are happy with the accommodation at an early stage when you can still make changes.

Complaints

Even with the best will in the world, you cannot please everyone. There will always be complaints, sometimes justified and sometimes not. It is how you deal with these that is important. Do not argue or lose your temper, even though you feel the visitor is wrong.

If they have a valid complaint, try to remedy it, if it is within your power. It may be, however, that their expectations were too high or they misread the brochure and feel that you should be providing more than you are. You can do nothing about the fact that the pub is too far away or the local shop is closed on Sunday but you should have warned them in advance. If you did, and they did not pick it up, then all you can do is be polite and try to help by providing something to tide them over or inform them where there is a shop open. If they haven't brought towels, for instance, and you do not provide them, you have a choice. Either you could help by providing them on this one occasion or you point them in the direction of a shop where they can buy them.

However if some piece of equipment is not working or something is broken, you should apologise and fix or replace it as soon as possible.

Continue to be as pleasant as you can even when sorely tried, as can happen in some instances. If you are really struggling to keep your temper, excuse yourself and walk away. Ask your partner to take over. If this is not possible, go back later and sort matters out when you have calmed down a little (and hopefully they have too).

Check points

The most important points here are:

◆ Attitude is of prime importance when dealing with guests, both before the holiday and while they are in your properties. Be polite and professional at all times but remember that the personal touch is also appreciated.

◆ When you greet the guests, welcome them to their cottage and show them around, briefly explaining anything necessary. Then leave them in peace to unpack and unwind.

◆ During their holiday, be responsive to the attitude of the visitor in judging how much contact to provide. Chat to them, be friendly and helpful but if they do not really respond, again, leave them in peace to enjoy their holiday.

◆ When your visitor is leaving, do not hurry them unless they are late, but be there to say goodbye.

◆ Most holiday cottage owners now provide a welcome pack of some sort. This need be no more extensive than some tea, coffee, milk and biscuits. You might wish to provide a shopping service for the guests with payment when they arrive.

◆ Provide extras such as bathmats, tea towels, kitchen towel, some washing and dish washing tablets if you find it reasonable to do so, but keep costs in mind and if it proves too expensive to maintain this, cut back.

◆ Information in the cottages should be kept up to date. You should consider providing:

- official tourism information;
- extra information on local walks, attractive car tours, etc that you could write yourself;
- information on local restaurants, bars, etc;
- essential contact numbers for doctor, dentist, hospital, garage, coast guard or mountain rescue (if applicable).

◆ Offer help to visitors who ask you to book events or activities (particularly if there are language difficulties). Can you provide assistance in times of emergencies?

◆ Do not expect your guests to pay for any surprise extras. You must inform them of any extra costs involved before they book their holiday.

◆ Do not behave in an intrusive way to the guests. Do not offer unwanted advice or knock at their door for a chat. Do not offer opinionated advice. Keep your children and pets from annoying the visitors too.

◆ Try not to get involved with disagreements between guests, either in different properties or in the same party. If the argument is between guests in separate properties, intervene only if you feel responsible in any way or if you can really help.

◆ Never enter a property when the guest is not present unless it is really essential. In the case of a visit from an official of some sort or a tradesman to do some work, warn the guest in advance. Stay with the official or tradesman at all times.

◆ Questionnaires can provide you with a valuable insight into guests' opinions on your cottages. Use an official version or draw up one yourself. Take note of the results and if you see recurring points, try to make the necessary changes to the properties.

◆ At some time or other you may receive a complaint from a visitor. If it is valid, then remedy it if you can. At all times be polite, keep calm and do not lose your temper.

PROGRESS PLAN

1. Make a note of any extras you might think of providing for your guests, including a possible shopping service. Make enquiries locally to see if any shops are willing to deliver groceries to your properties.

2. Start drawing up any personalised information you could provide on the area or walks and car tours round about.

3. From your own past experience of visiting properties, what extra items would you like to have if you were a guest?

4. Draw up a questionnaire you might issue to guests, including any particular points you might want to have guest opinions on.

In conclusion

The level of service you provide will influence the number of bookings you receive. You want to provide quality accommodation, where guests will be very pleased both with the overall atmosphere created and with the properties. Your attitude in the everyday dealings you have with the guests, and your willingness to help by putting yourself out to ensure that their holiday is a memorable one, will count highly with your visitors. Only you can assess the level of involvement you wish to have, and this may also vary from guest to guest. Judge each group of guests at face value and if any particular visitor seems to want to be left in peace, then let them.

Service is not servility. It is up to you to provide the service that will bring your visitors back again. It is your business and should be your pleasure – at least most of the time!

16

Keeping Up Standards

Your business is up and running and the visitors are holidaying in your cottages. You are providing an efficient and friendly service to your guests and everything is going well. What should you consider next?

It is of great importance now that you keep up your standards. Giving the properties a thorough clean after the visitor has left, carrying out an even more thorough spring clean every year, repainting as necessary to keep the décor up to scratch and renewing or repairing any damaged furniture and fittings should be your main tasks.

Cleaning

End of visit cleaning

This is not necessarily carried out weekly but must happen whenever a cottage is vacated at the end of a guest holiday period. This can be after a short break of a few days or perhaps on occasion after a fortnight. You and/or your cleaners will have only a few hours to turn the cottage round before the next guest arrives. It is a good idea to have a checklist of tasks, as it is all too easy to forget to do something in the rush. If you have more than one person helping then have certain assigned tasks for each of you or you will be repeating the same jobs.

Many guests leave the properties in an immaculate condition but you certainly cannot rely on this. Even if they do, you should still re-clean the cottages yourself to be on the safe side.

Your checklist for the property should include most of the following.

◆ **Change the beds**. If one room has been entirely unused, then it is fine to leave the bedding there but if even only one bed in a twin room has been used, you should change both. Most people leave luggage or clothes on the unused bed and it is less than fresh at the end of a holiday let.
  Put in clean towels if you provide them.

◆ **Clean out and reset the fire/stove if you have one**. Some guests will do this themselves and you will bless them for it. It should, of course, be done before the next job on the list.

◆ **Dust all surfaces**. This is especially important if you have an open fire or stove. Include the television screen here – it attracts dust.

◆ **Check for cobwebs**. Use a long-handled feather duster.

◆ **Clean the bathroom(s)**. This includes cleaning the bath, wash hand basin and the loo as well as the tiles and the floor. Clean the shower screen and replace any bathmats you provide. Put in a new loo roll.

◆ **Clean the cooker**. You have only a short space of time available, so you clean the top, the grill pan and the oven. You cannot deep clean the oven at this stage and it may not need it anyway. Take the opportunity, if you have a gap in bookings, to give the oven a more thorough clean. A dishwasher, if you have one, is very useful for getting the oven trays and shelves sparkling with the minimum of scrubbing.

♦ **Clean the kitchen**. The kitchen is the most important room in the property to keep as clean as possible. Surfaces, cupboards, windowsills, cooking equipment and floor as well as any breadbin, microwave and toaster and other equipment, must be cleaned. Check the cutlery and crockery, and clean fridges and freezers. Pay special attention to the glasses – they should be sparkling.

Many visitors leave food behind as they simply do not want to carry it home again with them. You will need to work out your own policy on this. We tend to leave any salt, pepper, oil, jars of dried herbs and tomato ketchup, but, of course, remove frozen food, bread, biscuits, etc.
Put in tea towels if you provide them. Replace the oven glove if necessary.

♦ **Check all light bulbs**. You can easily do this while you are cleaning. It is a good idea to have a small stock of bulbs in each property but there is no telling whether the visitor will use these. We have had a visitor wait until the last day to inform us that a bedside light was not working when all that was required was a new bulb. Check the stocks of extra bulbs in the properties from time to time as, for some reason, guests sometimes put the old bulbs back in the box rather than throwing them away.

♦ **Empty all bins and replace bin bags**. Leave some black bin bags in the properties for the visitors to use.

♦ **Sweep all floors and carpets**. Dog hairs are hard to get rid of, so use a heavy duty vacuum cleaner for the properties if you welcome animals.

♦ **Wash windows**. These should be sparkling inside and out. In the country, in rainy weather it is pointless to clean the outsides of the windows but it is a task you can do, if you need to, during the week, when the visitor may be out for the day.

♦ **Check thermostatic valves on the radiators**. Guests will turn these up or down as the temperature changes. Make sure they are all left at a suitable setting each week.

◆ **Check the television**. If you have had teenage boys in the property, you may find the settings of the television have been altered because they have been using Play Stations, etc during the visit.

◆ **Throw out remaining toiletries**. Remove any used soap, shampoo, shower gel, etc that guests may leave in the bathroom(s).

◆ **Clean mirrors**. Clean and polish the mirrors.

◆ **Air the rooms**.

Longer term cleaning

Freshening up the properties for the year ahead is essential. This deep cleaning should take place annually at least, though some of the following tasks should be carried out as often as is necessary.

◆ **Clean curtains**. Again, if you have an open fire all the furnishings in the room will get dirty much more quickly than if you rely on heating by radiators only.

◆ **Clean carpets**. These will have received heavy wear during the year and will probably need a good clean before the season gets into its stride. Get the professionals in or hire a carpet cleaner.

◆ **Wipe down paintwork and skirtings**. This should be done as often as is necessary during the year. In times of bad weather you will find the properties get very grubby and the cleaning needs to be more thorough.

◆ **Wash shower curtains**. Again this needs to be done several times a year. Have spare sets of curtains and put them through the washing machine regularly. The better quality shower curtains wash well. The poorer quality ones become hard and unusable after a few washings.

◆ **Dry clean duvets and wash bedding**. You will probably have different weights of duvets for winter and summer and can get one type cleaned while the other is in use. Wash mattress covers regularly and have spare ones available for emergency use. Replace pillows on a regular basis as they can become discoloured with constant use.

- **Clean cooker**. This is your chance to give the cooker a really good clean.

- **Sweep chimney**. This is vital in order to prevent falls of soot or at the worst, a chimney fire. It should be done at least once a year if it is in regular use. Get this done during the summer months, rather than waiting for the autumn when everyone else is getting theirs swept too.

- **Clean lampshades**. Wipe down all lampshades or replace them if necessary.

- **Clean skylights and less accessible areas**. This is your chance to reach those areas that are normally inaccessible. High ceilings above stairways, skylights and other difficult to reach places should be thoroughly cleaned at least once a year.

- **Check electrical plugs**. This is necessary for safety. It would normally be carried out by an electrician but you can buy an appliance through electrical suppliers which will do the job. (See Chapter 17 for more details.)

- **Check all crockery for chips etc**. Although you should be looking at these each week, take time to have a thorough check through all the plates, dishes etc for wear and tear.

- **Check dripping taps etc**. Again you can call in a plumber for the larger jobs or replace a washer yourself, if you feel confident enough to do so.

Repainting and decorating

However carefully you look after your properties they will begin to look shabby after a year of heavy use. Doors and skirting boards will get scuffed, walls and cupboards will be marked and paintwork generally will look less than fresh. You should try to keep a general rolling programme of redecoration in force throughout the properties, if you can. It is easier to deal with than the alternative of closing down while you redecorate everywhere, as well as being better for the pocket. At least you will have some income while you decorate if you can let the other properties at the same time.

If you started off with new or refurbished properties, these will continue to look good for quite a while, but if you took over a business which was already up and running, the time will come quite soon when you feel that some redecoration is needed.

The chances are that if you simply want to use the same colour again, you will find that it has been discontinued. Wallpapers, too, tend to go out of fashion in a few months. We started by keeping a note of the paint colours we had used in the different cottages but found it pointless, as so many of them were unavailable when we went back to buy some more. Either keep extra stocks of paint in the shed (these will not keep for ever), or be content to change the colours every time you repaint. Our cottages all vary enormously in shape and design and we have further emphasised this by using very different colours in each of them. This, of course, adds to our problems when we are repainting as we have to keep a stock of various different paints to touch up areas when we need to. If you go for plain colours everywhere, your job is made easier as well as cheaper as you do not have to buy a whole range of paints.

Even if you do not want to carry out a major redecoration programme, simply putting a fresh coat of paint on all the woodwork makes a real difference to a property. We always walk through the cottages at the end of a season and note any places where redecoration is needed, trying to see the properties through a guest's eyes. It is surprising how easy it is to miss signs of wear unless you are looking out specially.

Renewing furniture, bedding, etc

Buying as good a quality of furniture as you can afford at the start will pay off in the long run. With normal wear and tear, your sofas and armchairs should look perfectly okay for quite some time. As mentioned before, washable loose covers are an excellent idea for these.

There are the small items you will have to renew such as cushions, lampshades, pillows, bedlinen, crockery, cutlery, table mats, kitchen equipment, etc. And then there are the more expensive items which will be as follows.

White goods

Check washing machines, dishwashers, fridges and freezers regularly. Your guests will tell you soon enough if any of them are not working properly, but it helps to know yourself if a piece of equipment is coming to the end of its useful life. Visitors are probably not as careful with your goods as they would be with their own. Also the equipment is probably not exactly the same as they are used to at home so some mistakes can be made with the operation.

Electrical outlets will always try to sell you service cover with the goods. Just how worthwhile this actually is, is open to debate. In many cases it is more cost effective to simply buy a new piece of equipment. We have found it best to pick sturdy, uncomplicated but good quality goods. There seems little point, for example, in having an all-singing, all-dancing electronic washing machine for people on holiday. Most people only use a few basic programmes, if they in fact use the machine at all. As long as it does the job well and is easy to operate, then it is fine.

Carpets, rugs

Small rugs can be renewed cheaply but to re-carpet a large area of floor is expensive. A wool and man-made fibre mix lasts well in most areas. Laying a carpet in a bathroom is not recommended as it can become very damp and is therefore considered to be unhygienic. Carpeting close to an outside door will discolour quickly too and require frequent cleaning or replacing. You might consider tiling some areas instead as a long-lasting option, as tiles always look good and are easy to maintain.

Sofas, chairs, tables

As mentioned before, the direct selling sofa companies provide good value. Dining chairs with separate cushions can be brought up to scratch very easily with new seat covers.

Look in the small ads columns of your local paper for coffee tables, dining tables and chairs for sale as well as sofas and easy chairs. There are some surprisingly good bargains to be had. All foam used in upholstery must comply with the Fire and Safety Standards – so make sure that the appropriate labels are in place.

Beds

Sagging mattresses are not at all acceptable and nor are beds that are past their best. Mattresses should be renewed as often as necessary. The frequency depends on many factors including the quality, the usage and if any untoward accidents have occurred. Beds should last considerably longer if you choose a good quality at the start. It is probably not politically correct to say so, but people are getting larger and heavier. The beds need to be strong and as large as possible – king sized rather than double.

Garden furniture

Taking it inside in the winter months and treating the wood regularly will prolong the life of your garden furniture. You can pick up real bargains in garden centres at the end of the season. Choose sturdy cedarwood or similar chairs and tables for long-lasting life.

You do not want to have to replace several large items at the same time, so try to stagger your purchases. Buy at sale time, look in the small ads and use the direct selling companies.

Outside maintenance

The outside of your properties is important. Do not neglect it in favour of the inside. The properties should always be kept clean, well decorated and in excellent condition. The grounds and any gardens also need constant attention, especially through the summer months. Some of the tasks you need to address in order that your properties should always look their best are:

♦ **Lawns**. Keep the grass mowed and the edges neat. This is essential maintenance and should be carried out on a frequent basis.

♦ **Gutters**. Clean out the gutters to prevent them from getting blocked by leaves etc. Repair or replace any broken guttering as required.

♦ **Paintwork**. The paintwork on windows, doors and any brickwork or stone must be kept as immaculate as possible. If you are in areas where the weather is more extreme you may have to repaint more frequently, especially on walls subjected to the worst of the gales over the winter, for example.

- **Tiles/slates**. Check the roofs as you walk about the properties. Missing slates or tiles can cause a leak inside a property when it rains. Do you have a friendly roofer you can call on in an emergency?

- **Driveways**. Keep these free of potholes and weeds, and the edges in good order.

- **Flowerbeds/tubs, etc**. This is part of the decorative side of gardening. Keep the flowerbeds free of weeds and renew plants when the seasons change. Shrubs and roses are easy to maintain and do not need constant work. Try to choose plants and shrubs so that you have some colour in the garden all year round. Winter pansies and bushes with berries or those that flower in the cold months are useful.

- **Courtyards**. Keep these in good order and free from weeds. Repair any cracks and loose slabs or cobbles. These can be a hazard to you and the visitors alike.

- **Oil supply**. If you have an outside oil tank or gas cylinder, keep the area round it in good order and keep it out of the reach of the visitors. If you want to hide the supply, grow a climbing plant on a screen in front of or round the tank.

- **Sheds/outbuildings**. These, of course, should also be kept in good condition. They should be well-painted and neat with the guttering sound. If you live on a working farm, then allowance has to be made for the fact that there could be mud, animals and machinery around the place. This is inevitable.

- **Private water supplies**. There is very little maintenance involved with a water supply. Check the filters frequently and that the water is flowing into the tanks in sufficient quantity. Problems usually occur in the drier months and when the ground is frozen. Keep an eye daily on the situation at these times. It is not hard work, merely something you need to keep on top of. The secret with water supply maintenance is 'minor but regular' checks.

◆ **Private sewerage**. Again this is not difficult or time consuming. You will need to get the system cleaned out every so often, possibly every three years or so depending on usage. Either private companies or the local authorities will do this for a reasonable fee.

Check points

The following points are important to remember:

◆ The cleaning carried out when the visitor leaves at the end of their holiday should be thorough. In each room you should:
  – dust;
  – check light bulbs;
  – empty bins and replace bags;
  – vacuum, sweep and/or mop floors;
  – check radiator valves;
  – wash or clean windows.

Also you should:
  – clean and reset any fire;
  – thoroughly clean the kitchen and all equipment including the cooker;
  – change the beds;
  – clean the bathroom.

◆ Longer-term cleaning involves:
  – cleaning curtains, carpets and furnishings;
  – wiping down all wood – skirtings, doors, etc;
  – cleaning duvets and pillows, washing blankets;
  – sweeping chimneys;
  – checking electrical plugs;
  – checking crockery and cutlery;
  – dealing with dripping taps.

◆ Items of furniture and bedding should be renewed when necessary. This includes carpets, rugs, mattresses, sofas, chairs and garden furniture. It is debatable whether it is worth taking out a service contract on white goods such as refrigerators, washing machines, dishwashers, etc as this can be expensive. It may be that for most of the appliances it would be better to simply buy again from new.

◆ The outside maintenance of your properties is also important. Here you should be concerned with looking after:
- lawns;
- gutters;
- tiles and slates;
- driveways;
- paintwork;
- flowerbeds and tubs;
- courtyards;
- any private water supplies;
- any private sewerage;
- oil or gas supply;
- sheds and outbuildings.

PROGRESS PLAN

1. Draw up a full checklist for cleaning all your properties and if more than one person is to be involved in the cleaning, assign tasks to each.

2. Do the same for the outside, again assigning tasks that are to be carried out by particular people.

3. You may have bought all your furniture from new, bought over the stock with the business or your furniture may have been bought on a piecemeal basis, some new, some second hand. Walk round the properties and note any of the appliances, furniture or furnishings that you feel will need to be renewed in the near future. Work out some costings for this.

In conclusion

As the years go by and your business becomes fully established it is easy to let standards slip through neglect, lack of money or simply because you become a little blasé about the whole matter.

 **TOP TIP** ◆

> Every now and then, walk round the property as though you were a visitor. Keep an objective eye open for parts of the building you have rather neglected.

Look out for shabby sections of the property, for poorly maintained areas of the gardens, for broken slates, cobbles or brickwork.

Walk through the cottages themselves. Note the furniture that you had previously thought would do for another year. Will it really? Have a close look at the carpets. Check the tiling in the bathrooms and the paintwork everywhere. Test the electrical equipment in the kitchen and elsewhere – toasters, microwaves, etc.

Best of all, take a friend with you and ask for their help in spotting those necessary tasks. Draw up a list of the jobs you have seen that need doing and items that will need replacing. Separate the list into a section for each cottage and then the outside. When you have done that, break down each section into short-term and long-term tasks and, very importantly, start carrying out the short-term tasks immediately. You cannot afford to let standards slip.

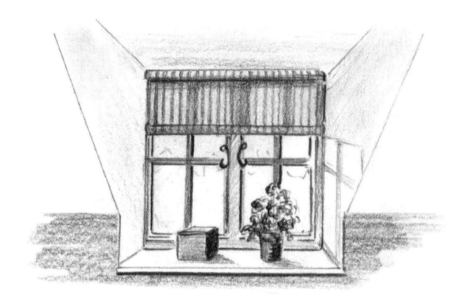

17

Knowing the Regulations

There are certain statutory regulations of which you need to be aware as the owner of a self catering business. There are also rules that you will have to abide by, chiefly for insurance purposes. It is important that you follow any necessary regulations and keep in touch with new developments on the legal front that apply to the holiday cottage business world. It is also useful to know how to deal with any emergencies that may arise on your premises or among your guests.

For Scottish self catering businesses, the Association of Scotland's Self-Caters has a website which includes a series of useful guidance notes for members, covering several of the points in this chapter.

Fire

Fire is a wonderful friend and a dangerous enemy. Fire can kill. As an owner of holiday premises you have a responsibility to your visitors to make sure that you do your utmost to fulfil all your obligations to keep them safe. There are several factors to consider.

Fire extinguishers and fire blankets

Every individual property should have a fire extinguisher and a fire blanket placed in a prominent position in the kitchen (between the cooker and the door) or kitchen area. It is not good enough for them to be in a kitchen cupboard. All fire extinguishers should have either the British Standard kite mark or a European CE mark on them. These extinguishers do not last forever. It is possible to have a contract with a company to inspect them annually, but otherwise they should be replaced regularly as the pressure in them drops after a number of years. It is also advisable to have a separate extinguisher near the top or bottom of the stairs.

If your property is not of straightforward construction with a door to the outside then you might need fire safety signs and a plan with all the marked fire exits.

Smoke detectors

Each individual property should have at least one smoke detector installed in it. There are two kinds: those that are battery operated and those that are hard wired into the electrical system. In larger premises there is sometimes the requirement to link detectors so that one triggers all. Batteries, in the first kind, can last a number of years, depending on the make. They emit an insistent beeping sound when the batteries require replacing. Smoke detectors that are wired in are more expensive and should be connected by a qualified electrician. They will have battery backup to cover power failures.

If you are building new holiday cottages, converting a building into holiday cottages or carrying out any building work at all on the properties, building regulations will state that you should install an interconnected, hard wired system of smoke detectors in each property. This links the alarms, causing them all to sound in an emergency.

Carbon monoxide detectors

If your stove or open fire is not burning efficiently, it may be producing carbon monoxide fumes. Carbon monoxide detectors look similar to smoke detectors but are a little more expensive. There is no general statutory requirement for these.

Furniture

The Furniture and Furnishings regulations set levels of fire resistance for upholstered furniture, furnishings and other products containing upholstery. These regulations apply to furniture in holiday cottages. The furniture affected by these regulations is:

◆ armchairs, sofas, dining chairs (including any loose or stretch covers);
◆ beds and divans;
◆ sofa beds and futons;
◆ children's and nursery furniture;
◆ cushions and pillows.

What is not affected are:

◆ duvets and bed linen;
◆ mattress covers;
◆ pillowcases;
◆ curtains;
◆ carpets;
◆ sleeping bags;
◆ goods made before 1950 and any materials used to re-upholster them.

All new furniture bought since March 1990 should meet with these standards already and should have labels to prove it.

Detailed guidance on the regulations and on furnishing properties generally is available in the booklet 'A guide to the furniture and furnishings (Fire) (Safety) regulations', published by the Department of Trade and Industry. You can obtain this booklet from the Trading Standards Office.

Utilities

Gas safety regulations

The Department of Trade and Industry Gas Appliances Regulations state that manufacturers should affix an approved type 'CE' marking on all gas appliances and supply a fitting certificate if relevant. These confirm that the appliance complies with EC regulations. 1994 legislation states that any property with a gas appliance, particularly a gas fire, must be inspected and serviced by a CORGI (Council for Registered Gas Installers) plumbing and heating engineer at least every 12 months.

Carbon monoxide (CO), a lethal colourless, odourless gas, is a by-product of burning fuel and its commonest source in the home is gas fires, boilers and solid fuel appliances. Poor insulation of the appliance, poor servicing, damage or poor ventilation can cause the gas to build up to dangerous levels. The Health and Safety Executive produces leaflets on gas safety but for any advice you can contact the Gas Safety Action Line on 0800 300 363.

Electrical safety

As the holiday cottage owner you are responsible for the safety of your guests with regard to the electrical appliances that you provide for them such as:

♦ vacuum cleaners;
♦ electric fires or radiators;
♦ toasters;
♦ cookers;
♦ microwaves;
♦ washing machines;
♦ dishwashers;

- fridges;
- freezers;
- sandwich makers;
- electric coffee makers;
- hair dryers;
- mixers;
- kettles;
- irons;
- TVs;
- lamps;
- radios;
- videos, DVD and CD players.

There are checks that you should make on a regular basis as some visitors will not treat the equipment in the cottages as well as they might. After switching off and disconnecting the plug, check for any obvious signs of damage or wear such as:

- cuts and abrasions on the cables;
- cracked plug casings;
- bent pins;
- outer covering loose where it enters the plug;
- coloured insulation on wires showing through.

Also all plugs should be checked and passed as safe. It is a good idea to keep a record of electrical testing that you carry out.

Government regulations now limit the sort of DIY work that can be carried out on your property. All domestic electrical installations are classified as 'notifiable' and 'non-notifiable'. You as an amateur can still do minor 'non-notifiable' work such as replacing accessories (including socket outlets, control switches and ceiling roses) except if it is in a high risk area exposed to water – the kitchen, bathroom or garden. Most other work has to be done (or inspected and certified) by a competent person. If it is not, the owner of the property must give notice to the local authority building control department which will inspect the work.

It is much wiser to hand over all electrical work to a qualified electrician.

Selling electricity on to the visitor

You have the option in your properties of including the electricity in the total cost of the week's rental, of charging by meter reading or of installing a coin operated meter. Different owners prefer different solutions. If you decide to charge the visitor directly, either by meter reading at the beginning and end of the holiday or by a coin operated system, then there are regulations you must abide by.

The maximum price you can charge your guests is equivalent to the standard single domestic tariff charged by the local electricity company in your area. It is inclusive of VAT (at the lower rate). Part of it is the maximum amount you can charge for each unit of electricity used by the visitor and the rest is a daily 'availability charge' for providing the supply. This latter part is supposed to cover the installation cost for the meter and wiring, and the cost of a fixed standing charge.

If you decide to include the cost of the electricity in the weekly rental, the maximum price outlined does not apply. It does not apply either in the situation where a flat rate for electricity is charged over and above the rental price.

Private water supply

Some properties in the more remote areas will have their own water supply. The local Environment Health Department has a duty to check the quality of the supplies in their area. Most holiday properties will be tested once a year and a register is kept of all the private supplies together with the test results. You should make it plain in your brochure and on your website that the cottages are fed by a private supply which is tested regularly.

The Department will inform the owner in advance that a Health Department officer will be calling to test the supply. The testing is quick, but a charge is made for the visit and for the analysis of the water sample. Coliform (bacteria) is the most common form of water pollutant.

After a couple of weeks the results will be sent to you with any recommendations necessary. It is advisable, as mentioned before, whatever the results, to install an ultra-violet disinfector with filter, which zaps any bacteria which may pass through the pipework. This has the advantage of providing a pure drinking water supply without any chemicals being added. These units are initially expensive but fairly inexpensive to maintain, only requiring periodic replacement of the filter and the ultra violet tube.

Health and safety

If you employ anyone in your business, for example to help with the cleaning on a changeover day, you must meet the minimum workplace standards for employees. Most of the legislation is really for businesses employing staff on a more permanent basis but you should be aware of any responsibilities that you might have to the staff you do employ. Most of it is common sense, but it is as well to check for the following:

◆ Carrying out a risk assessment. If you have a larger business you should make sure you know of any areas where the employees might be at risk.

◆ Providing clean toilet facilities for employee use.

◆ Meeting fire safety standards.

◆ Ensuring employees know how to work any equipment safely.

◆ Reporting accidents to the relevant authorities.

For more information on this topic, check the website www.businesslink.gov.uk.

Employment regulations

Standard minimum wage

The adult minimum wage will be increased from £4.85 to £5.05 in October 2005 and the intention is to further increase it to £5.35 in October 2006. For 18 to 21 year olds the minimum wage will be increased from £4.10 to £4.25 in October 2005 with a further increase to £4.45 in October 2006. The minimum wage for 16 and 17 year olds is £3 at present and will remain under review. The website www.dti.gov.uk/er/nmw will give you the current rates at any time.

Migrant workers

The Home Office has a website with information on the rules affecting migrant workers, including the checks needed to prevent the hiring of illegal workers. The site is at www.employingmigrantworkers.org.uk.

E-Commerce Regulations

The Electronic Commerce (EC Directive) Regulations have implications for most businesses that have commercial websites i.e. those that are not for personal use only. Those regulations cover three main areas:

◆ *You have to provide information on your website to enable users to identify you.* This means that you need to show:
  - the name of your business;
  - your geographical address;
  - an email address;
  - details of membership of any trade organisation;
  - details of membership of any supervising scheme e.g. a quality assurance scheme;
  - VAT registration number (if applicable);
  - prices with what is included and any extras.

◆ *If you have a site which gives people the chance to buy services, e.g. booking online, more information must be provided.* You then need to provide:
  - all the steps required to conclude the 'contract';
  - whether or not the 'contract' e.g. the booking, will be 'filed' by you;
  - the code of conduct relevant to the transaction – the Secure Server ID;
  - terms and conditions relevant to the transaction (in an easily downloadable form);
  - all transactions are to be acknowledged electronically without 'undue' delay.

- *In relation to e-marketing* any unsolicited or solicited marketing material must be identified as such. You, as the sender, must also be identified clearly, as should any special offers you make.

Then there are the other important issues covered in the Regulations such as liability for intermediate service providers. For more information on the E-Commerce Regulations go to www.dti.gov.uk.

Dealing with a death on the premises

Let's hope that this will never happen but it is as well to be prepared in case it does. If one of the guests is reported to you as having died, your first task is to phone the doctor. The doctor will then take over the proceedings. The patient will very probably not be known to them, so by law they must report the death to the police.

The police, when they arrive, will interview everyone involved and take statements from them. They will also arrange for the deceased to be moved to the local morgue to await the decision of the authorities. In Scotland, if the death does not seem to be suspicious at all (for example, if the person was elderly or ill) then a death certificate will be issued by the Procurator Fiscal. If the death is totally unexpected a post mortem will be carried out to determine the cause.

In England and Wales a sudden death means that there automatically has to be a Coroner's court hearing.

What can you do through all this? All you can do is offer comfort and assistance to the bereaved. Showing a quiet sympathy and simply being there to listen will be a help to them. They may want a minister or priest to be involved, so it is probably wise to have the relevant contact details for these available. You may also have to show a flexibility towards booking arrangements, where this is possible.

It is only sensible to have the telephone number of the local undertaker available. In Scotland, once the death certificate has been issued, the undertaker will take charge and deal direct with the families concerned.

Insurance

Specially designed for self catering operators, your insurance policy could cover all of the following.

* Accidental damage cover on contents and buildings, including damage by holidaymakers and other occupants.

* New for old on contents.

* Theft cover (not subject to forcible entry).

* Public and employer liability, covering claims by employees and by guests.

* Loss of revenue due to damage, defective sanitation, pollution, etc.

* Glass: this includes events such as plate, sheet and laminated glass and sanitary ware breakages.

* Money: this should cover the loss of money in the form of cheques and cash.

You may be expected to pay an excess sum for some of these items. For more details of insurance cover for self caterers, contact one of the insurance companies listed in the Appendix.

Data Protection Act

In order to process bookings and meet any special requirements you, as an owner, need to use the information provided by the guests such as name, address, email address, telephone number, any special needs such as those for guests with mobility problems. You have a duty, under the Data Protection Act, to protect this information from being divulged to others unless by the consent of the guest. However, as you would not normally be passing any information about guests to a third party, this is not hard to comply with.

If, however, you decide to build up on the computer a data bank of information concerning your guests, perhaps those who are 'regulars', then the position is a little more difficult. By the terms of the Act, strictly speaking the guests should be informed that you are amassing this information and so be able to ask for a copy at any time. You are then duty bound to give them this. Again, it is your responsibility that it does not fall into the hands of others.

It is difficult to see how this would work in reality. If you are making a simple list of names, addresses, pets and likes and dislikes, this seems innocuous enough and a guest might think it strange if you informed them of it. It is as well to be aware of the pitfalls however, and to act with caution. Do not make any comments in writing that could be considered offensive, even though that is not your intention.

Check points

It is important to be aware of the many regulations that can affect you, as a self caterer, in the different areas of your business.

- In the case of fire, you need to know about:
  - fire extinguishers and fire blankets;
  - smoke detectors;
  - carbon monoxide detectors;
  - rules governing furniture and furnishings.

Detailed guidance on the regulations is available in 'A guide to the furniture and furnishings (fire) (safety) regulations' published by the Department of Trade and Industry. Also consult the fire officer at your local fire station for advice.

- To comply with the Gas Safety Regulations, all gas appliances should have an approved 'CE' marking on them and a fitting certificate if applicable. For advice on gas safety contact the Gas Safety Action Line.

- With electrical safety in mind, you should make regular checks on all electrical appliances, plugs, etc in the properties now that the regulations for electrical work are more stringent. You as an amateur can still do minor 'non-notifiable' work such as replacing accessories, except if it is in a high risk area exposed to water e.g. the kitchen. Most other work has to be done (or inspected and certified) by a competent person.

- If you are selling on electricity to the guests, the maximum price you can charge your guests is equivalent to the standard single domestic tariff charged by the local electricity company in your area. It is inclusive of VAT (at the lower rate).

- Will you have a private water supply? If so it must be checked annually by the local Environment Health Department. A charge will be made for the visit and the testing. It is advisable to install an ultra-violet disinfector to ensure the safety of the water.

- You are responsible for the health and safety of the guests and any employees you have while they are on your premises. Most of the requirements, such as clean toilets for employees, making sure the cottages do not hold any particular hazards, etc are common sense.

- You should check the current rates for the National Minimum Wage if you will be employing staff.

- If you decide to employ migrant workers, check the Home Office website for guidance: www.employingmigrantworkers.org.uk

- The Electronic Commerce (EC Directive) Regulations have implications for most businesses that have commercial websites i.e. those that are not for personal use only.
  - You have to provide information on your website to enable users to identify you, such as name, address and details of membership of any trade organisation.
  - If you have a site which gives people the chance to buy services, e.g. booking online, more information must be provided. This includes the terms and conditions of the transaction and the code of conduct relevant to the transaction amongst others.

- Dealing with a death on the premises is never a pleasant prospect. First of all the doctor should be contacted and will take over from that point. Procedures are different in the different parts of the UK. Your most important role will be to comfort the bereaved.

- Your insurance policy should be specially designed for self caterers and cover accidental damage, theft, public and employer liability, loss of revenue due to damage, etc and the loss of money (cheques, cash, etc) in the course of your business.

◆ You have a duty under the Data Protection Act to protect any information you hold about your guests from being divulged to any third party. If you have built up data on your visitors they have a right to know this and to ask for a copy at any time.

PROGRESS PLAN

1. Make a list of all the regulations that will apply to your business and research the sources of information on these. Make sure you know exactly what is involved in complying with any of these.

----

2. Draw up a plan for testing electrical apparatus in the cottages, listing all relevant appliances with dates tested. Make a simple visual check now.

----

3. Check that your business website fulfils all the e-commerce regulations. If it does not, then what do you need to do to make it compliant?

----

4. Which of these regulatory areas would you consider to be most complex? What assistance might you seek in getting clarification of it as regards your business?

Where do you stand?

Rules, regulations, legalities – these are all important when running a business. It is necessary to be aware of any commitments you have to employees, to be cognizant of legal requirements you have to meet and to know where you stand on EU rulings.

Having said all this, much of it is common sense and, for example, just as you would naturally make sure that all your electrical appliances were in good working order in your own home, so you would expect to do the same in your holiday properties. For the very small business, as the majority of self catering businesses are, although there are legal requirements to meet these need not be too arduous. If you are at all in doubt about your legal liabilities or the rulings you need to comply with you should check with the relevant authorities.

18

Business Matters

Working from home is a new experience for many people. Setting up an office is the practical side of the matter but the discipline involved in sitting at a desk and getting your records organised, when the sun is shining outside, is much harder. Running a self catering business is not a full-time occupation, however, and there is plenty of time for a walk by the river or a coffee in the garden when the weather is good. There is also the opportunity of doing those necessary outdoor tasks. This is all part of its charm for us.

Then there is the more official side of business life – tax, National Insurance, VAT and business rates. They may not all affect you or your business but it is necessary to be aware of them and to know how to find out any information you might need concerning them.

First of all let us consider the setting up of your office. It may be that you have a sufficiently large enterprise to have a separate building for this, but it may be that a room in your house is all that is required. Ideally, if it is to be in your house, you should try to lay aside a dedicated area, preferably a room you can close the door on, to set up your workspace.

Setting up an office in your home

Working from home involves the following.

Establishing a separate workspace

It is possible to set up a computer and some office equipment in the corner of your sitting room, or under the stairs, but this has some real disadvantages. If you have young children, for example, leaving paperwork, letters, cheques, etc around is asking for trouble. Depending on your frame of mind also it is either too tempting to get drawn into doing other things or to get into the habit of going back in the evenings to carry on with some work.

So, if possible, set aside a separate room where you can shut yourself in and concentrate on what you are doing and then leave at the end of a work stint and close the door on everything.

Designing or acquiring facilities to enable you to work efficiently

As a self catering business you do not need a large number of facilities in your office – just the furniture which will make your job easier. This probably means:

◆ a desk with space around it to move;
◆ a comfortable chair for working;
◆ good lighting;
◆ a filing cabinet or filing unit;

- shelves for books etc;
- workspace for spreading things out;
- technological equipment (see later).

Think about the positioning of electrical sockets when you are setting up. Trailing leads can cause a safety hazard. It also helps the concentration if the office is warm in the winter months, so some form of heating is necessary.

Keeping on top of your paperwork

You need to establish a system and stick to it. If you and your partner are dividing the necessary work between you, then you should work out a system and keep to it. If you are the one who is responsible, for example, for recording all the bookings or sending out the letters of confirmation, make sure that you do it. This does not mean that you sit back, having completed all your tasks, and watch him or her working on into the evening! You are both running this business and so should be helping each other when necessary. But it is all too easy for jobs to be forgotten or letters misplaced when there is no clear responsibility set out for certain tasks. At least, with a clearly divided workload, you both know whose fault it is if anything is left undone!

You should make an effort to be efficient in taking bookings and dealing with enquiries. Give yourself a set time limit in confirming bookings, sending out brochures, answering queries, etc.

Check your email regularly. If there are enquiries, answer them straightaway if you can. As emphasised before, keep files up to date, entering invoices on a regular basis. Register bookings, deposits and balances when received and do not just leave the letters in a pile to deal with later.

◆ TOP TIP ◆

Keep a handwritten list of 'things to do' which you can constantly update when you think of anything new or complete a task.

Being firm with yourself when there is work to be done

You will not need to work in the office every day. Or, at least, if your schedule is to work a couple of hours in the mornings only, then make sure to stop after that and give yourself some free time. One of the joys of working from home with your very own business is that you can decide when to work and when to stop working, without feeling guilty. Part of your business consists of talking to your visitors or checking the water supply or going into town to buy some goods – a new lampshade, some paint, or tea and coffee for the welcome pack.

On the other hand, when you need to get some important administration done, do it there and then. Get the letters ready for the post or work out the wording for the advertising you need to send off by a fixed date. Do not put off essential tasks or those with a time limit.

Being able to switch off when the time comes

This is not difficult. If the sun is shining or your partner wants to go out for the day and you haven't really got any essential tasks to complete, why not go out and enjoy yourself? If the business is not suffering, there is no problem.

If you have a dedicated reception/office building on a larger self catering site, it must of course always be manned in working hours. This makes getting away more difficult as either you or your partner will have to be on site during office hours. This makes trips out together during the day impossible, unless you can employ someone on a temporary basis to look after the office for you.

In the evenings make time for the family and for other things in your life. Just because the computer is always available does not mean that you always have to use it.

Building up tradespeople and suppliers you can trust

This is a very important factor in your business. If you carried out any building work at the beginning then you would have perhaps employed joiners, builders, glaziers, electricians, plumbers and tilers. Keep a note of the names and telephone numbers of any of these that you felt did a good job and were not too expensive. Keep an ear to the ground locally for other tradesman who are recommended by neighbours or friends. All this will pay off when you need a plumber or tiler in an emergency.

Acquiring and learning how to use technology

There is so much technology around that you can guarantee there is something out there that is perfect for your needs. There is also the great temptation to buy more than you really need. For your business you should be looking at purchasing a:

- computer with various software packages and internet access;
- printer;
- scanner;
- copier;
- telephone system;
- fax (possibly).

If you have broadband in your area you will find it very useful. If not, it is perfectly possible to run a successful business without it. Your computer should have top grade antivirus software on it. This is not expensive to buy and can be downloaded from websites or uploaded from a CD. The computer virus is a constant menace and you are particularly vulnerable as you will be receiving a stream of emails daily as part of your business, largely from people you do not know. Most of the viruses seem to strike through the email, many of them sending out spurious new emails based on your electronic address book. As this is automatically updated with an address when you reply to a new email, the list of addresses is an ever growing one unless you take steps to constantly delete old addresses. You may become the innocent link in receiving and distributing this virus.

There are various different combinations of the copier/scanner/printer/ fax setup. Look into these thoroughly before you put down your money. What will be important to you? If you are going to create your own brochures you need a good quality colour printer. If you are going to be taking your own photographs for publicity purposes you will need a good quality scanner or a digital camera with software to load the results into the computer. Do your homework first. When you are considering a printer, for example, do not be seduced by the low cost of the machine. Find out first the prices of the replacement cartridges. Some are horrendously expensive. Look out, also, for the ones that have a simple colour cartridge for all three primary colours. This can be wasteful if you print with a bias towards one colour – the cartridge will require replacement when this single colour runs out.

As for phones, you will probably have a mobile, handy for calls when you are out and about, though of limited use in some country areas like ours where the reception is poor and spasmodic. Digital systems with base units and remote pre-registered handsets can be used in different locations round your property, reducing the need for additional wiring. It is all a matter of what is useful to you and what you prefer.

Business rates

Most businesses pay business rates but exactly how much your business will pay depends on a number of factors including the location of your property and how you are using it. You will probably have to pay business rates on your self catering business and possibly on using your home as an office. The system for calculating these rates, and the small business relief you might apply for, varies.

Your regional assessor will ask you for detailed information regarding your business before making an assessment of your business rates. They will send you a valuation which will also be used by the relevant water authority to produce the water and sewerage rates. If you wish to appeal, you need to write to the assessor within six months of receiving your evaluation.

The office in your home
If you have set up one of the rooms in your house as an office for running the business, there is always the possibility of having to pay business rates on this part of your property (as well as the actual letting cottages,

of course). Usually, you would only pay business rates on an office in your home under certain conditions. These would include the extent and frequency of the business use of the room and any special modifications made to the property. This is unlikely in an office serving a self catering business, so you will probably be exempt.

Each case is decided individually and you should consult your local Valuation Office for further details if you are concerned about it.

Renting out a holiday home

If you have a holiday home you only have to pay business rates on the property if you plan to make it available for rent for at least 140 days a year. Otherwise you pay council tax. If you do not make a conscious decision to restrict bookings to 139 days or less your property is liable for a business rates assessment regardless of the number of days you actually let it out.

The larger self catering business

If you have a self catering business involving several cottages, the same applies as to the situation above.

Small business rate relief

This varies depending on which part of the UK you live in. In England and Wales (2005 figures) your self catering business may be eligible for small business rate relief. Businesses with rateable values of below £5,000 will get 50% rate relief on their liability. This will decrease on a sliding scale of 1% for every £100 of rateable value over £5,000, up to £9,999. This relief is available to ratepayers with either one property or one main property and other additional properties, providing the additional properties do not have individual rateable values of more than £2,200, and the combined rateable value of all the properties is under £15,000 (or £21,500 in London). The threshold for the combined rateable value depends on where the main property is.

As well as this relief, eligible businesses with rateable values of between £10,000 and £14,999 (£10,000 and £21,999 in London) will have their liability calculated using the small business multiplier. You must apply for the rate relief each year and be eligible on April 1 of each year.

In Scotland the Scottish Executive has introduced business rate relief for small businesses as rate payments account for a larger proportion of the costs of small businesses than for those with a larger turnover. All businesses with a rateable value of £10,000 or less are eligible for a discount of between 5% and 50% on the rate poundage. The percentage relief increases with the decrease in rateable value of the non-domestic property. If the rateable value is £7,000 or above it is 5%, £6,000 and under £7,000 – 10%, £5,000 and under £6,000 – 20%, £4,000 and under £5,000 – 30%, £3,000 and under £4,000 – 40%, and less than £3,000 it is 50%.

The exact level of relief depends on the total rateable value of all the properties owned by the rate-payer and whether or not the property is eligible for one of the existing non-discretionary rate reliefs.

If you live in Northern Ireland you are advised to consult your local authority for advice or one of the companies which provides business advice for small businesses.

Tax and National Insurance

◆ How you deal with tax and National Insurance depends on whether your business is a limited company or if you are acting as a sole trader or in partnership.

Limited company

If your business is a limited company you will be a director of that company. As such, you are considered an employee of the company, and you will pay tax through Pay As You Earn (PAYE) and National Insurance (Class One) (NIC) by deductions from your gross salary. The company will also have to pay an element of NIC for any employees you have. You must register your company as an employer with the Inland

Revenue (0845 6070 143 – helpline for new employers). You will then receive a pack of documentation containing all the material you need to calculate and deduct PAYE and NIC.

If you employ others you are responsible for deducting PAYE and NIC when their earnings reach certain weekly levels. Inland Revenue Business Support Teams can provide you with free payroll support if you are a small and new business.

Sole trader or partnership or self-employed

You must register your business for both tax and National Insurance purposes within three months from the start of trading, or a penalty of £100 (at 2005 figures) for late registration will be levied. You can register by phoning the new helpline for the self employed on 08459 154515 or by completing form CWL1 from your local Inland Revenue enquiry centre. When you have registered you will be sent a guide 'Cutting through the red tape – The right way to start your business'.

You are excluded from paying NIC if you are a man aged over 65 or a woman of over 60, or if your business profits are less than £4,025 (at 2005 figures) or if you are under 16.

Otherwise you will be charged the basic Class Two contribution. If the taxable profits from your business exceed £4,615 (at 2005 figures) you will also be charged Class Four contributions. Class Four contributions are paid along with your tax assessment. If you work for an employer and also run a business in your spare time, you could be liable to pay Class One, Two and Four National Insurance Contributions though there is an upper limit on the amount of NIC you have to pay in one year.

You will also be required to complete an annual Self Assessment Tax return giving details of all income received during the tax year, including your business income. The penalty for late entry of this form (after 31 January following date of issue) is £100 at present. Again, the Business Support Team of the Inland Revenue will give advice with regard to keeping records, allowable/disallowable business expenditure and how to fill in your tax form.

VAT

Value Added Tax is a tax on consumer expenditure. It is collected on business transactions, imports and acquisitions. Most business transactions involve supplies of goods or services and VAT is payable if they are:

◆ supplies made in the United Kingdom or the Isle of Man;
◆ by a taxable person;
◆ in the course of a business;
◆ are not specifically exempted or zero-rated.

You can find out details of which goods and services may be zero/reduced rate or exempt on the Customs and Excise website (see Appendix).

Should you or should you not register for VAT? If your business has a turnover of more than £60,000 per year (2005 figure) you are legally required to register. The main advantage in registering is that you can claim back the VAT you pay on all your business purchases, but this means that you must keep very accurate records. As a VAT registered company you become a tax collector for the government. You can also charge VAT on any products and services you supply which are **positively rated** at 17.5%. Some products such as gas are chargeable at a reduced rate.

If your annual turnover is under £60,000, you have the option of registering if you wish. If you decide not to register this is by far the easier option. It means that you cannot claim back any VAT you have paid out on supplies for your business but it also means that you do not have to worry about charging VAT on bookings, etc. Any VAT on bookings must be part of the overall cost of the week's holiday and should not be added as an extra for the visitor.

If you have not registered for VAT because your business turnover is too low, but feel that it will grow to a figure over the limit eventually, it is a good idea to start separating out the VAT from the prices you pay for goods from the start. This will give you a clear idea of exactly how much VAT you are paying over the course of a year and will prepare you for the day when your business might grow enough to meet the limit. The switch to recording VAT will be all the easier when the time comes.

However, you should register when you think you are nearing the threshold. Usually VAT is paid quarterly although it may be worth enquiring about options if this is not convenient for you. From the moment you register you must keep accurate records of all VAT you have paid and all the VAT you have charged on your bookings. At the end of each quarter you should be able to balance out your two total amounts of VAT. If you have charged more on sales than you have paid on purchases you will be liable for the balance to the Customs and Excise. If it is the other way round you will be owed money.

There is a flat rate scheme for small businesses which simplifies VAT accounting procedures in an effort to save you time and money. It enables small businesses to calculate their VAT payment as a percentage of their total turnover. This scheme is open to businesses whose annual taxable turnover does not exceed £150,000. Details of this scheme are in Customs and Excise, Notice 733 – The Flat Rate Scheme for Small Businesses.

VAT on long lets

This only applies if you charge VAT on your bookings. Whether or not you must charge VAT on long lets depends on a number of factors:

- the type of let;
- the time or year;
- the site of the property;
- whether it is advertised for holiday letting.

If you are registered for VAT, letting your property for any period of time as long as it is for a holiday obliges you to charge VAT on the rental.

If the let is for longer than four weeks and the purpose is other than for a holiday, for example as a residential let, you will probably be letting it at a reduced rental. If so the whole letting period could be exempt from VAT. Whether it is or not depends on where your business is situated. If you are in an area where the holiday season was thought to be limited to a certain number of months of the year, if the let was 'out of season' and for business purposes it would probably not be liable for VAT. If, however, you are in an area where the holiday season is considered to extend throughout the year, then the let at any time would be deemed VAT liable. Basically, a 'business' let of longer than four weeks in what would be a 'holiday' period is always considered liable for VAT.

It is wise to consult the Customs and Excise Office in all circumstances as each case is assessed individually.

Check points

There are a number of important points to emphasise from this chapter.

- It is important, when setting up an office, either to establish a separate work space in your own home or to use a separate building altogether. This enables important paper work to be kept away from other members of the family and to be accumulated all in the same place.

- There are a number of facilities, in addition to the technology, you will need for this office:
  - desk;
  - chair;
  - lighting;
  - heating;
  - filing cabinet or unit;
  - shelves;
  - flat work space.

- Establish a system for dealing with the paperwork between those involved and stick to it as closely as possible. Keep a written list of 'things to do' available to update as required.

- Do not be tempted to neglect any work that needs to be done. If there are essential tasks such as getting an advertisement ready for a deadline, make sure these are carried out on time.

- Know when to switch off. Self catering is not a full-time business and if you can get away on occasion, then do so. It is also important to set aside some part of the day for other activities.

- Build up a list of tradesmen you can trust, are not too expensive and who you know you can rely on to help in a crisis.

- You will need a certain amount of technology in your office:
  - computer;
  - printer;
  - scanner;
  - copier;
  - telephone system;
  - fax.

  You will also need anti-virus software – buy the best as it is essential that your business does not become infected or pass on the virus to your visitors.

- You will have to pay business rates for your cottages if you plan to let them out for at least 140 days a year, but you may be able to claim small business rate relief. This varies with the location of your property – England, Wales, Scotland or Northern Ireland. You should ask your local authority for details or check on the websites of companies which provide advice for small businesses.

- How you deal with tax and National Insurance depends on whether your business is a limited company or you are acting as a sole trader or in partnership.

- As a sole trader/partner/self-employed person you must register your business for both tax and National Insurance purposes within three months from the start of trading, or a penalty of £100 (at 2005 figures) for late registration will be levied. You will be charged the basic Class Two contribution. If the taxable profits from your business exceed £4,615 (at 2005 figures) you will also be charged Class Four contributions.

◆ If your business is a limited company you will be a director of that company. You are also considered an employee of the company and you will pay tax through Pay As You Earn (PAYE) and National Insurance (Class One) (NIC) by deductions from your gross salary.

◆ You should register your company for VAT if it has a turnover of more than £60,000 per year (2005 figure). If you have a turnover less than this you have the option of registering. You will be able to claim back the VAT you have paid on all purchases for the business but you will have to charge VAT on all bookings.

◆ There is a flat rate scheme for small businesses which simplifies VAT accounting procedures and enables small businesses to calculate their VAT payment as a percentage of their total turnover. This scheme is open to businesses whose annual taxable turnover does not exceed £150,000.

◆ Even if your business is VAT registered, you may not have to charge it on all long lets. Each business is assessed on its own merits but, if the let is for over four weeks, the purpose is residential or business and you will be charging a lower than normal rent, it may be that the whole period could be exempt, especially if the let was out of season in a seasonally driven area.

PROGRESS PLAN

1. Make a list of all the furniture and major equipment you would need to purchase for your office. Investigate the costings:

_____

_____

3. Make a list of all the administration jobs necessary and divide the responsibilities between or among you.

_____

_____

3. Look up the relevant websites and send for information on any of the following that you think might be important for you:

_____

_____

In conclusion

Working from home as a sole trader, a self employed person or the director of a limited company brings with it increased responsibility. You are no longer someone who is paid by an employer at the end of the month and has someone else to work out all that tax, National Insurance and VAT. It is now up to you, either personally or in conjunction with your accountant. You need to be informed about new rulings on these topics, too, so should keep a watching brief on any websites that you find useful for information purposes.

Joining a trade association can help, as they are alert to any changes and should inform their members of matters relevant to self catering.

19

Maintaining the Momentum

Now that your business is going well, your properties are in excellent order and the bookings are coming in thick and fast, you might be feeling that there is very little else to consider. The work of converting the buildings and setting up the properties is long over. The marketing strategy and the advertising have gone well and you have managed to keep within budget. The feeling of excitement at the beginning of a year, as the weeks start to get booked up, is fading. Your list of return guests is long and you are feeling confident about the financial future of your venture.

How will you maintain your interest over the coming years if the whole project is not to become a chore? Somehow, the thrill of seeing an idea working in reality is not the same as maintaining that reality over a length of time and still keeping a sense of pride and interest in the whole venture.

You also have to consider the fact that as the years go by, ideas change and fashions come and go. Visitors will expect more for their money and will go where they can get what they want. You might have to think about adding new facilities or expanding into fields you would never have imagined before.

You could decide to ignore all this and simply keep going with the business as it is. If you do this, there may come a time when you have had enough, and it is at this point, or just before it, that you need to review your future. The easiest option could be to sell the business. If you have looked after the properties and the business well, there will always be people who are interested in taking over a successful self catering venture. If you decide you want to stay after all, then you will have to change and adapt, and above all keep yourself motivated in the coming years.

Keeping yourself motivated

First and foremost you should still be enjoying your life. If the changeover day is tiring and you find some guests irritating but you still love living where you do; if you still enjoy chatting to most visitors, and are proud of your properties; if you are still finding new ways to market your business and you discuss future projects with your partner from time to time – then you are doing well. But if you have begun to dread the changeover, if you are starting to avoid the visitors when you can or if you are becoming bored with your project, you need to keep yourself more motivated. How to do this? There are several ways and you can use all or some of them. You will probably be able to think of some new ways yourself too.

Consider the following.

Taking a holiday

This sounds very obvious but many people find it difficult to let go and trust someone else to run the business while they are away. It *is* difficult, but unless you have a break you will become very jaded. Is there a friend who you think might be interested in having a holiday in your house while also being willing to look after the cottages for a week? When you were in full-time employment you would not have considered working month after month without having time off. This is no different even though you are no longer travelling to an office and sitting behind a desk all day. A change of scene is good for you whatever your circumstances.

If you feel that you simply cannot afford it, have a look on the internet. There are so many cheap flights to warm places in the off season, where you can relax for a week, or exciting city breaks in Europe and beyond.

It may not be a rest you need but simply a break with routine. If you travel out of season, as you probably will want to, there are bargains to be had. Another consideration is to try to swap holiday accommodation with other cottage owners. You might be able to come to some agreement on an *ad hoc* basis or perhaps there is an organised 'swap service' for self catering property owners available.

You can always stay in touch with the business by phone if you really feel you need to.

Taking an awayday

This does not replace the need for a holiday. You can take an awayday at intervals when you are feeling fed up or when you simply need a change. This is definitely not a day out for shopping. Choose somewhere, from a road map if necessary, that you may not have been before. Wait for a day of good weather and simply go... Take a picnic or go for a pub meal. Visit an attractive village you have never seen before, take a trip round a castle or stately home or just go for a ramble or hill walk in peaceful countryside or along the shoreline. Above all make an effort not to discuss business. A day out is like taking a bath. It refreshes you for a while and you feel a lot better but the feeling does not last. You need to keep on taking them!

Draw up a list of trips you would like to make in the year. Fix the sheet of paper onto the fridge door with a magnet and refer to it when you are feeling a little jaded or if the sun is shining. You do not have to wait until you are desperate.

There will be those of you who have a larger self catering operation and have to man the reception desk during office hours. Can you find someone else to do the job for the odd day? Otherwise you will have to take time off when you can – perhaps in the long summer evenings after hours.

Having another life

You may have been concentrating full-time on your business to the detriment of your social life or even to the detriment of any other life! The old saying about 'Jack being a dull boy' still applies. Do you find yourselves talking about the business if you go out for the day or when you are sitting about in the evenings? Do you talk about anything else? If this is sounding a bit like you, then you must rouse yourself to do something different. Building up a social life is an obvious start. You no longer have work colleagues so it is even more important to make an effort to find friends in the area, particularly when you are spending the larger part of every day in the company of your partner.

Can you split up sometimes and each go your separate ways for a day, or take up something new? Why not develop an interest into a hobby – archaeology, basketmaking, amateur dramatics, line dancing, etc. Find an interest of your own and join a club or go to classes. There are so many opportunities around wherever you live. Being apart for some of the time will improve your relationship. You will have something new to talk about for a start!

Joining a trade association

You will need some motivation in the business side of your life too. Joining an association of people who are all working in the self catering industry will give you and your business a real boost. Going to local meetings and attending the AGMs will give you a deeper insight into all matters affecting self catering and will enable you to influence, through the association, the decisions made by the National Tourist Boards. Talking to people with the same problems as you can also bring out new solutions to those problems and give you new ideas to follow. You can also update your skills through various tourism-related training courses which may be available through these associations.

You will make new friends too. The association will have opportunities for advertising and you can learn, through the experience of others, where and how it is best to advertise your business.

You might also find someone who is prepared to carry out a 'property swap' for that important week's holiday. Or you could organise a group within the association who would be prepared to exchange properties on a recurring basis.

Large scale refurbishment

This is not something you would undertake lightly. Refurbishment on a large scale is expensive and you have to consider the cash you have available. You need to be customer focused. This will justify certain expenditure but you cannot afford to go wild. In any refurbishment programme you have to match the super-duper with the strictly practical. Do not get carried away by taking out large loans that you will be struggling to repay – and spending sleepless nights worrying about! At the very least, weigh the benefits gained from the refurbishment against the financial return. Will it bring in more guests? Will you be able to put up your prices because of the new facilities? Are you entering a profitable new market?

You will have the same sort of considerations as you might have when you are planning a major refurbishment of your own home. Is it worth it in financial terms? Will it give you a higher price when you sell it? If not, is it worth carrying it out? Estate agents can give you the answer to that, but in the self catering business you may have to use your own initiative or ask those in a similar position.

It may be, of course, that your refurbishment has been dictated by your continuing membership of a letting agency. In which case you have little choice if you wish to continue using the agency.

If your plan is to respond to current trends such as installing more bathrooms, putting in luxury facilities such as a jacuzzi or a sauna, or giving your guests the opportunity of broadband facilities in the cottages, you should be able to raise your prices to regain some of the costs involved. If however you want to bring older buildings up to date by putting in good insulation, renewing windows or doors or replacing a kitchen, it is unlikely that you can recoup this. If it is strictly necessary, as the buildings are not up to scratch in your eyes, then so be it. You will simply have to go ahead, but consider how long you will take to repay any loan with your current rate of income.

New ideas

This is where you can use your imagination to think laterally. Your business has been working quite satisfactorily for a number of years but you are beginning to feel that something new is needed. Perhaps you feel that introducing some interesting ideas such as workshops, craft courses, games facilities or a different kind of holiday programme would revolutionise your income and give you a new interest.

The sort of new ideas you have after a convivial session at the pub are not necessarily ones which will stand the test of time, so mull them over for a while and discuss them with anyone who is in the same business and might have tried one or two of them.

What might you consider as an innovative idea for your business?

Adding to the number of properties

You might think about adding a new cottage, lodge or chalet to the number you already have. This is perhaps an obvious thought but you could build something completely different. What about an environmentally friendly property, specially advertised as such, and very intriguing for the growing market classed as 'the green visitor'?

Promoted separately from your other properties, this could command higher weekly rates and provide a focus for your business.

Alternatively you could convert or build a cottage in keeping with the area you live in, such as a black house in the Western Highlands, or a thatched cottage in Wiltshire or a traditional style fisherman's cottage on the east coast. Again these should be advertised as such. Unique buildings such as these are increasingly popular with visitors who are willing to pay to live for a week in very special surroundings.

Then again there are the new and stylish wooden lodges with decking balconies and large windows, which, sited overlooking a view, are particularly appealing.

Workshops and courses

There are an enormous number of courses on the market now, many of them running over a week, though some are for longer. They include:

◆ practical courses in photography, cooking, china mending, weaving, basketmaking, etc.

◆ artistic courses in painting, sculpture, music, art appreciation, architecture;

◆ historical courses in archaeology, local history, genealogy;

◆ spiritual courses in meditation, visualisation, inner peace, dowsing, crystal healing;

◆ outdoor courses in climbing, abseiling, canoeing, sail boating.

And so many more. Your property will not be suitable for all of these and you will not be interested in them all but perhaps, if you have a large enough space in a games room or barn or even in one of the holiday properties, you might consider running a course for a few days to see if it is viable.

You do not have to run it yourself but you will be expected to provide meals during the day while the course is in progress. Whether you decide to put everyone up in the cottages or give them a list of suitable B&Bs in the area is your decision. If you are putting people up you will be charging for the accommodation as well as for the course. You could try this in the quiet season when you do not expect to have any guests normally. Advertising on your website and in suitable publications or in the newspapers should bring enquiries.

You can provide meals without becoming a 'restaurant' officially, if you restrict the number of times per year in which you run residential events.

If you belong to a club or craft association which might be interested in attending a course, you are well on the way to success as you can contact them direct.

New kinds of holidays

The tourism world is changing year by year. It used to be that people came to a cottage for a fortnight in the summer or a week at any other time. Nowadays visitors are more flexible with their plans. There are still those who come for a fortnight but more often it is a week – and not only in the high season. People are taking their holiday entitlement in different chunks, perhaps a main holiday abroad in the summer but then a week either in the spring or the autumn, closer to home.

◆ **TOP TIP** ◆

Consider getting together with other self catering owners and advertising a two-centre holiday, one week in your cottage and one week in theirs.

Or would you consider setting one of your cottages aside to be booked on a nightly basis with a two or three nights minimum stay? You could continue booking the others on the more usual weekly basis.

Have you thought about running 'learning' holidays? You can see them advertised frequently in magazines – 'Spend a week in Tuscany and learn to cook the Italian way'. This is not quite the same as the one or two day course mentioned before. You might think of setting aside a few of the cottages for a week at a time for guests who want to come on a photography holiday or one where they are learning to paint with water colours, for example. If you have a skill to teach them yourself, then this would be a bonus, but it is possible to find people who are experts in their field and who would be willing, for a fee of course, to teach a group for a week. The cost of the tuition for the guests, would be in addition to the normal cost of the accommodation.

Then there are all those activity holidays advertised by the Tourist Boards and by local organisations: cycling holidays, fishing holidays, climbing holidays, walking holidays, golfing holidays, etc. Could you provide accommodation for one of these? Could you advertise your properties as suitable for golfing or fishing holidays in the area, for example? You could also check with the local tourist office to see what they were promoting and perhaps follow their lead.

Refining your market

After a number of years, or even earlier if you feel that you are beginning to know your market better, you should seriously think about refining this market. The world changes, fresh ideas grow stale, tourism widens its market in the world and plans which seemed good at the time become unworkable.

Check your National Tourist Board. They often have initiatives on marketing and advertising that you might find useful. Do you look at their website on a regular basis? It might be worth checking it to see if any of the plans they have for the next year could be useful to you.

You cannot afford to let other businesses steal a march on you. Your business is part or even the whole of your livelihood and you want it to succeed and continue succeeding. Marketing is the way you present your business to the world and you need to keep on top of it.

There are several ways you should be doing this.

Cutting out dead wood

You can download useful software to count the number of hits you receive on your website and to record where they come from. Some of the sites you have been advertising on will have their own hit counter, sometimes for each webpage advertisement. Use this information to cut out any dead wood, i.e. any sites where you are paying for advertising but which are not giving you a worthwhile return. You have probably been advertising on many websites that offered a free advert for the first six months or so and then asked for a fee for any future advertising. Is it worth paying that fee? Check the website to see how self catering is represented. Sometimes it is obvious that the site has been created chiefly for the serviced sector of tourism and has added on self catering as an afterthought. Stop using it.

Does the holiday website you are using feature near the top of a search with the major search engines? If it does not you could be wasting money advertising with them.

The same argument applies to magazines and newspapers. Are you really getting a good return on these? If your advertising is not bringing you the visitors, do not use it anymore. It sounds obvious, but sometimes inertia can creep in and when that sales person from the advertising department phones to give you a good price for a series of advertisements for the coming year you just agree. Instead, be ready for them. Have your statistics worked out in advance and do not be seduced into advertising unnecessarily. If you are getting a fair return but you are not overly impressed, cut down the number of advertisements per year. Be prepared to negotiate as well – they will often drop the price, if pressed.

Are there facilities you provide that are not really making any difference to your guests? Are there goods in your welcome pack, for example, that the visitors always leave untouched?

Check how effective your website and brochure are

Do you ask your visitors when they book a holiday with you how they came to hear about your business? If they have seen your website, have you asked how useful they felt it was? Feedback from visitors is the easiest way to find out how effective your advertising is. If they seem reluctant to tell you, stress that any comments they make will prove useful to you for the future. You can count the number of hits you have on the site but you cannot assess from the site alone how informative it is for the visitor. If you are getting similar answers from several people then you should consider changing or updating your site to reflect these comments.

Perhaps, too, looking around the web you will realise that your site is now appearing rather out of date. There are always new and dynamic ideas around in design and, in booking their holiday, your visitors will have seen some very up-market websites for other properties.

You do not want to compare badly with these. Maybe it is time to have a new website designed. Research the market and check for other tourism orientated websites, especially those with interesting features such as a 360 degree tour of the properties. Would your business benefit from a completely new site, perhaps with an online booking facility, or in different languages?

Are you featured on the best search engines? Try some searches yourself using key words that you imagine a prospective holidaymaker would use in looking for a self catering property in your area. Is your site featuring on the first or second page? If you are down round about page five or lower, it is time to review the key words you use on your site.

You will have changed your brochure over the years too, but have you thought about a complete overhaul? If you have always created it yourself on the computer, what about approaching a printing company to see what they can suggest?

Change or add markets

Perhaps you have targeted walkers, golfers or the family market. Is your strategy still working? If not, it is time to change. Contact the local Tourist Board to find out if they promote holidays for any particular markets. If these do not coincide with your choice you might be targeting the wrong people. You should consider changing your market.

Then there is the other side of the coin. What sort of visitors are you getting at present and how can you encourage more of them? Are they part of the market you were planning for? If not, you need to adapt your strategy to attract more of them.

You may need to broaden your marketing plan. Are there new fields in your area that you can exploit? Perhaps an activity centre has opened or a major sporting event will be taking place in your area in the future. Contact the organisers and find out details, asking about advertising opportunities and a possible accommodation list.

Respond to current marketing trends

New ideas and trends in tourism are coming out year by year. The major Tourist Boards develop strategies to attract visitors of all sorts but there are definite areas in which they feature current trends. It helps to be aware of these areas. At present they are promoting the rise of 'green tourism', encouraging environmentally conscious visitors to come to Britain.

Can you promote your business on these lines? Can you make any changes to the properties or the grounds that will bring you those 'green' visitors?

The market for activity holidays is increasing. Are there opportunities in your area for these activities? Feature them in your marketing and advertising where the young and active holidaymakers will take note.

Look out constantly for new marketing initiatives and, if you can, respond to them.

Respond to worldwide changes

The fear of growing terrorism has driven away American visitors who are only now starting to return to Britain after the events of 11

September. If USA guests were a large part of your business you will have suffered badly in the interim.

The foot and mouth epidemic caused real hardship, not just among the farmers whose animals were slaughtered, but among the many businesses relying on the tourist for a living. Large parts of the countryside were out of bounds for weeks. The tourism businesses that were located in the affected areas, and those which simply were in or near to the country anywhere in Britain, suffered a dramatic downturn in visitor numbers.

How can you deal with these disasters? You can do nothing about the basic situation, the lack of visitors and the shrinking market that result. You need therefore to be aware of the possible effects they have and to be ready to switch to new markets as soon as possible. Flexibility is important. If, for example, visitors from the USA are important to you, put that side of the strategy on hold while you explore other avenues. Can you attract more European visitors or more from this country? What is the Tourist Board doing to bring in more business to the country? Find out about the campaigns they are running and where they are holding roadshows or attending exhibitions abroad. Maybe you can use them to further your own advertising. Contact your local Tourist Board.

The opening up of Eastern Europe as a tourist market (as well as a tourist destination) has created a possible whole new tranche of visitors to Britain. With the many cheap flights, new ferry routes and increased ease of travel for these countries, there is a widening European market available for your business. Is there some way you can directly reach this new market?

Go up market

Have you considered going up market? Find out from your local Enterprise Agency whether grants would be available for raising the standard of your accommodation. You will get a sympathetic ear as most tourism influenced agencies are interested in raising the standard of holiday properties in their area. With your more up-market accommodation you can attract a new kind of visitor and your prices should be raised accordingly.

Check with your Quality Assurance Advisor to see what is needed to bring your business up to the star level you want. If you feel the outlay is worth the new business you will be getting, then go ahead.

Listen to visitors

What points have your visitors been making on the questionnaires they have completed? Is there a consistent theme throughout? If it is a criticism or a lack in facilities, you should consider remedying it if you can. Your visitors are your livelihood, so listen to them if you want them to return.

They may suggest a new market for you, a new form of advertising, amendments to your website or possibly that you could provide some service that would prove useful to them while they are on holiday. Whatever they suggest it is worth considering. If it would be too expensive or too difficult to implement, then you may decide against it. Keep it in mind however for a future occasion where you might have money available or you might need to increase your market.

Check your prices and what you are offering

Do not necessarily raise your prices year upon year without checking the market for similar properties to your own and seeing what they are charging. Are your prices all-inclusive? Many self catering owners charge extra for electricity, dogs, high chairs, etc and have priced their properties accordingly. If you provide heating and electricity, for example, as part of the package you may have to review the situation. In the winter months prices fall – that is the nature of self catering accommodation – but the heating costs rise. Are you charging enough in these months? Visitors expect low prices at this time of year but you may have to raise them a little to make winter letting viable for your all-inclusive package.

Do you provide all the bedlinen and towels? Again, some property owners charge extra for these. Are you giving your visitor value for money? They will vote with their feet if you are not.

Work with an agency

If you have always gone it alone but feel that the enquiries and booking side of things is becoming a burden you might consider putting your cottages in the hands of an agency. Agencies vary. You have the choice of more or less putting all the advertising, marketing and bookings in their hands or of using them as an adjunct to your normal service to boost bookings.

Ask other self catering owners you know who run a similar size of business to you, and use an agency, to recommend one to you. Then contact that agency and some others to compare charges, advertising campaigns and the service they provide.

Accept shorter bookings

There is a noticeable trend in the self catering industry towards shorter bookings. And not only shorter bookings but many more last minute bookings. Are you willing to respond to this trend? Perhaps you could lay aside certain months outside the main season in which you would welcome these holidays. Or you might consider accepting short breaks at the last minute for those gaps you have in high season.

The main difficulty is that the break concerned is usually over a weekend, thus eating into two weekly bookings. Short breaks during the week are not so much of a problem. However, with this trend set to continue you will have to seriously consider your strategy towards the shorter holiday.

Check points

This last chapter looks to the future, emphasising the importance of not becoming complacent. The main points here are:

- ◆ It is essential to keep yourself motivated if you are to succeed in the future. You can do this by:
  - – taking holidays;
  - – taking awaydays;
  - – having another life outside the business;

– joining a trade association.

♦ Large scale refurbishment is not something to be considered lightly. It is an expensive option but can reap dividends if it is successful in attracting a whole new market. However you need to balance the benefit against the costs involved.

♦ New ideas can bring a breath of fresh air into the business. Consider some of the following possibilities:
- building some new and different cottages, perhaps environmentally friendly or radically stylish ones;
- running workshops or courses;
- planning new kinds of holidays such as two-centre breaks or those where you learn a new skill.

♦ After a number of years you should be thinking about refining your market. It is time to:
- cut out deadwood such as advertising which is too expensive or no longer working;
- check how effective your website and brochure are, perhaps giving them a complete overhaul;
- change or add to your markets if your marketing strategy is not working;
- respond to current marketing trends;
- respond to worldwide changes by being one step ahead of the herd;
- go up market and raise the standard of your accommodation to bring in a new visitor with more money to spend;
- listen to visitors and respond to their comments;
- check your prices and what you are offering;
- work with an agency to release some of the pressure and to bring in new visitors;
- accept shorter bookings, perhaps in one cottage only, but all year round.

PROGRESS PLAN

1. How are you going to keep yourself motivated? Can you come up with some suggestions as to how you can stay interested in the business? Make some plans.

_____

_____

2. Perhaps you have been trading for a number of years now. What new ideas can you come up with to move your business forward? Work out the costs involved.

_____

_____

3. How are you going to refine your market? What will you cut out, what will you change and what will you add?

_____

_____

Your future in self catering

Do you have one? Or perhaps the question should be 'do you want to have one?' You have been building up the business over a number of years and now it has probably reached a plateau. Being realistic, you know the maximum income you can expect from your business. Is it sufficient for you? Have you considered any alternatives?

If you do want to continue you will need to take a long clear look at yourself and the business. I have considered in this chapter how to keep yourself motivated and what you can do to bring the business forward in terms of new ideas, improved facilities and new markets. I have also stressed that it is important to get rid of dead wood, to discard those ideas which seemed to work for a while but no longer do so and amend or redesign marketing tools such as websites and brochures which might now appear dated.

You might have a lot to do once you have considered your options, but this is part of running a business. You must meet demand to be successful – and the demand comes from your visitors. Listen to them and if what they say makes sense do something about it.

If you are sure that your future still lies in the self catering world, consider the old adage 'adapt and survive'. Good luck!

Appendix

Advice on setting up and running your business

There is a great deal of useful advice available for business start-ups, some of it directly relevant to the tourist industry. The advice covers a wide field including finance, marketing, grants and tax.

From banks
Some of the major banks offer excellent advice on their websites for planning and setting up a small business.
www.bankofscotlandbusiness.co.uk
www.ukbusiness.hsbc.com
www.natwest.com/smallbusinesses

From the Tourist Boards
Some tourist board industry websites are better than others at providing advice on starting up and developing a tourism business. Scotland and Wales, particularly, provide extensive assistance and advice.

England:
www.tourismtrade.org.uk
Provides marketing advice.

Wales:
www.wtbonline.gov.uk
Provides toolkits for both start-up and development.

Also contact the Business Support Team
029 2047 5303
business.support@tourism.wales.gov.uk

Scotland:
On www.scotexchange.net
Provides advice on starting your own tourism business and how to develop it further.

Northern Ireland:
www.nitb.com
Provides a start-up guide for self caterers.

From agencies and organisations
Business Link
Practical help and advice for small businesses in England. This covers workplace standards, starting up a business, finance and grants, employing people, IT and e-commerce, marketing, etc.
www.businesslink.gov.uk

Business Gateway
A service provided by the Scottish Enterprise Network and its partners to give a single access point for integrated services for businesses in Scotland. It provides information on starting up your business, book-keeping, data protection, tax and NI.
www.bgateway.com
www.sbgateway.com

Local Enterprise Agencies
www.scottish-enterprise.com

Highlands and Islands Enterprise
www.hie.co.uk

Local Chambers of Commerce
www.chamberonline.co.uk

The Business Eye Office (looking out for Welsh business)
Provides free and impartial information for businesses in Wales on finance, marketing, tax, IT, etc.
08457 96 97 98. www.businesseye.org.uk

Planning permission and building regulations
For England and Wales:
www.businesslink.gov.uk

For Scotland:
www.scotland.gov.uk

And the Enterprise Agencies:
www.hie.co.uk (Highlands and Islands)
www.scottish-enterprise.com (rest of Scotland)

For Northern Ireland:
www.planningni.gov.uk

Grants
Small Business Service's R&D Project Grant Scheme
www.businesslink.gov.uk

Local Development Agencies and Councils
www.grantnet.com

Enterprise Agencies
www.hie.co.uk (Highlands and Islands)
www.scottish-enterprise.com (rest of Scotland)

For tourism businesses in Wales
www.wtbonline.gov.uk

Setting up an office
Where to find furniture for the office.
www.office-world.co.uk

For all your office stationery, ink cartridges and much more.
www.viking-direct.co.uk

This site will provide a comparison of the tariffs of electricity, gas and telephone providers and calculate the savings you could make.
www.uswitch.com

Accounting software packages

MYOB (Mind Your Own Business)
Software designed for small businesses. First accounts package for start-ups and self-employed.
www.myob.co.uk

Simply Books
Easy to use package for very small businesses and small traders.
www.simplybooks.net

Legislation

There are a number of websites offering information on different forms of legislation. The Tourist Boards sometimes give advice also.

For Wales:
For general advice on issues such as fire safety etc for your business.
www.wtbonline.gov.uk

For Scotland:
For general advice on legislation affecting tourist businesses.
www.scotexchange.net

Health and safety information

www.hse.gov.uk
08701 545500

Fire precautions

Contact your local fire service.

The environment
www.environment-agency.gov.uk
0845 9333 111 (for Northern Ireland 028 90 540 540)

Data Protection Act
www.dataprotection.gov.uk
01625 545745

VAT information
Customs and Excise National Advice Service.
www.hmce.gov.uk
0845 010 9000 (0845 010 0300 in Welsh)

Business Gateway
www.bgateway.com

Business Link
www.businesslink.gov.uk

Tax and National Insurance
E-business helpline for information about internet services for Self-Assessment, PAYE and electronic filing of returns.
0845 605 5999

Helpline for the self employed.
0845 915 4515

Employing people. A helpline for new employers which provides guidance on aspects of National Insurance including income tax and payroll for new employers.
0845 607 0143

A helpline for existing employers on all aspects of National Insurance including general PAYE information and basic registration.
0845 714 3143

For information on paying tax and NI for your business:

For England contact Business Link.
www.businesslink.gov.uk

For Wales contact Business Eye.
www.businesseye.org.uk

For Scotland contact Business Gateway.
www.businessgateway.com

UK business rates
For official information on business rates in England and Wales, including renting out a holiday home and using your home as an office:
www.mybusinessrates.gov.uk

For Scotland:
The Business Gateway website.
www.bgateway.com

Rate relief for small businesses
For information and examples illustrating the small business rate relief scheme in Scotland.
www.scotland.gov.uk/library5/finance

And the Business Gateway.
www.bgateway.com

For England and Wales.
www.mybusinessrates.gov.uk

Disability
Official website www.disability.gov.uk

The Disability Rights Commission
08457 622 633

Text phone: 08457 622 644

enquiry@drc-gb.org

www.drc-gb.org

DRC Helpline, FREEPOST, MID 02164, Stratford upon Avon CV37 9BR

Greener environment

For energy efficient buildings:

The Solar Trade Association for all information on solar energy, etc. 01908 442 290. www.greenenergy.org.uk

The British Photovoltaic Association for information on photovoltaic systems. 01908 442 291. www.pv-uk.org.uk

To find out more about the various eco-friendly systems available and a list of contacts, get in touch with the Centre for Alternative Technology. 01654 705 950. www.cat.org.uk

Or Clear Skies (who will also advise you on the grants available). 08702 430 930. www.clear-skies.org.uk

Insurance for holiday cottages

Schofields Underwriting Agency, Lloyds Bank Chambers, Market Place, Bury BL9 0QL. 0161 7972915

J. L. Morris, Insurance Brokers Ltd., 1 Market Close, Poole, Dorset BH15 1NQ. 01202 649330

National Tourist Boards

Britain and England

Consumer website

www.visitbritain.com

Tourism industry website

Website: www.tourismtrade.org.uk

VisitBritain, Thames Tower, Blacks Road, London W6 9EL. +44 (0) 20 8846 9000. Fax: +44 (0) 20 8563 0302

Wales
Consumer website
www.visitwales.com

Tourism industry website
www.wtbonline.gov.uk

Wales Tourist Board, Brunel House, 2 Fitzalan Road, Cardiff CF24
   0UY. 029 20499909. Fax: 029 20485031

Scotland
Consumer website
visitscotland.com

Tourism industry website
www.scotexchange.net
VisitScotland, Ocean Point One, 94 Ocean Drive, Edinburgh EH6 6JH.
info@visitscotland.com 0131 472 2222

Northern Ireland
Consumer website
www.discovernorthernireland.com

Tourism industry website
www.nitb.com
St Anne's Court, 59 North Street, Belfast BT1 1NB. info@nitb.com
   +44 (0)28 9023 1221. Text phone: +44 (0)28 9089 5512

Tourism Organisations in England

Regional Tourist Boards
Cheshire and Warrington Tourism Board, Grosvenor Park Lodge,
   Grosvenor Park Road, Chester CH1 1QQ. 01244 346 543.
   info@cwtb.co.uk www.visitcheshire.com

Cumbria Tourist Board, Ashleigh, Holly Road, Windermere, Cumbria
   LA 23 2AQ. 01539 444 444. mail:@cumbria-tourist-board.co.uk

www.golakes.co.uk

East Midlands Tourism, c/o Mike Baulcombe at EMDA, Apex Court, City Link, Nottingham NG2 4LA. 0115 988 8300

East of England Tourist Board, Toppesfield Hall, Hadleigh, Suffolk IP7 5DN. 01473 822 922. www.eetb.org.uk

England's North Country, Renaissance House, PO Box 37, Centre Park, Warrington WA1 1AB. 01925 400362. www.enctrade.com

Heart of England Tourist Board, Woodside, Larkhill Road, Worcester WR5 2EZ. 01905 761100. info@hetb.co.uk www.hetb.co.uk

Isle of Man Tourism, Department of Tourism and Leisure, Sea Terminal Buildings, Douglas IM1 2RG. 01624 686 801 tourism@gov.im www.visitisleofman.com

Jersey Tourism, Liberation Square, St. Helier JE1 1BB. 01534 500700. info@jersey.com www.jersey.com

Lancashire and Blackpool Tourist Board, St George's House, St George's Street, Chorley PR7 2AA. 01257 226600. www.lancashiretourism.com

Marketing Manchester, Churchgate House, 56 Oxford Street, Manchester M1 6EU. 0161 237 1010. www.destinationmanchester.com

One NorthEast Tourism Team, Aykley Heads, Durham DH1 5UX. 0191 375 3000. enquiries@ntb.org.uk www.tourismnortheast.co.uk

South West Tourism, Woodwater Park, Pynes Hill, Rydon Lane, Exeter EX2 5WT. 0870 442 0830. post@swtourism.co.uk www.swtourism.co.uk

The Mersey Partnership, 12 Princes Dock, Princes Parade, Liverpool L3 1BG. 0151 227 2727. www.visitliverpool.com

Tourism South East, 40 Chamberlayne Road, Eastleigh, Hampshire SO50 5JH. 02380 625 400. enquiries@tourismse.com www.tourismse.com

VisitGuernsey, PO Box 23, St. Peter Port GY1 3AN, Guernsey. 01481 726 611. enquiries@visitguernsey.com www.visitguernsey.com

Visit London, 6th Floor, 2 More London Riverside, London SE1 2RR. 020 7234 5800. enquiries@visitlondon.com www.visitlondon.com

Yorkshire Tourist Board, 312 Tadcaster Road, York YO2 2HY. 01904 707 961. info@ytb.org.uk www.yorkshiretouristboard.net

Tourism organisations
Tourism Alliance, Centre Point, 103 Oxford Street, London WC1A 1DU. +44 (0)20 7395 8246. www.tourismalliance.com

Self catering associations
The English Association of Self-Catering Operators (EASCO). info@englishselfcatering.co.uk www.englishselfcatering.org

Cumbria and Lakeland Self Caterers Association (CaLSCA), Hazelwood Court, Lindale Road, Grange-over-Sands, Cumbria LA11 6SP. 015395 34196. www.lakesbreaks.co.uk

Other useful organisations
Federation of Small Businesses, Head Office, FSB, Sir Frank Whittle Way, Blackpool Business Park, Blackpool FY4 2FE. 01253 336000. www.fsb.org.uk

Tourism in Wales

Regional partnerships
North Wales Tourism Partnership
07831 597408
www.tpnw.org

Mid Wales Tourism Partnership
01654 704220
www.tpmw.co.uk

South West Wales Tourism Partnership
01558 669091
www.swwtp.co.uk

Capital Region Tourism Partnership
029 20417194
www.capitalregiontourism.org

Tourism organisations
Wales Tourism Alliance
www.wta.org.uk

Self catering associations
Wales Association of Self Catering Operators (WASCO)
wasco@walescottages.org.uk
www.walescottages.org.uk

Local Tourism Associations
For current contact details see the Wales tourism trade website:
www.wtbonline.gov.uk

Other tourism companies
North Wales Tourism (NWT)
www.nwt.co.uk

Mid Wales Tourism (MWT)
www.mid-wales-tourism.org.uk

Tourism in Scotland

The area network
Aberdeen and Grampian
Suite 3, Exchange House, 26/28 Exchange Street, Aberdeen AB11 6PH.
    01224 288828. www.aberdeen-grampian.com

Angus and Dundee
21 Castle Street, Dundee. 01382 527527.
www.angusanddundee.co.uk

Argyll, the Isles, Loch Lomond, Stirling and the Trossachs
Old Town Jail, St. John Street, Stirling FK8 1EA. 01786 445222.
www.visitscottishheartlands.co.uk

Ayrshire and Arran
15A Skye Road, Prestwick KA9 2TA, 01292 678100.
www.ayrshire-arran.com

Dumfries and Galloway
64 Whitesands, Dumfries DG1 2RS. 01387 245550.
www.visit-dumfries-and-galloway.co.uk

Edinburgh and the Lothians
4 Rothesay Terrace, Edinburgh EH3 7RY. 0131 473 3600.
www.edinburgh.org

Greater Glasgow and the Clyde Valley, 11 George Square, Glasgow G2
1DY. 0141 204 4480. www.seeglasgow.com

Highlands of Scotland
Peffery House, Strathpeffer IV14 9HA. 01997 421160.
www.highlandfreedom.com

Kingdom of Fife
Haig House, Balgonie Road, Haig Business Park, Markinch KY7
6AQ. 01592 750066

Orkney
6 Broad Street, Kirkwall, Orkney KW15 1NX. 01856 872001.
www.visitorkney.com

Perthshire
Lower City Mills, West Mill Street, Perth PH1 5QP. 01738 627958.
www.perthshire.co.uk

Scottish Borders
Shepherd's Mills, Whinfield Road, Selkirk TD7 5DT.
www.visitscottishborders.com

Shetland
  Market Cross, Lerwick, Shetland ZE1 0LU. 01595 693434.
  www.visitshetland.com

Western Isles
  4 South Beach, Stornoway, Isle of Lewis HS1 2XY. 01851 701818.
  www.witb.co.uk

Organisations and associations

Scottish Enterprise, 150 Broomielaw, Atlantic Quay, Glasgow G2 8LU.
  0141 248 2700.www.scottish-enterprise.com

Business Gateway
0845 609 6611
www.bgateway.com

Highlands and Islands Enterprise, Cowan House, Inverness Retail and
  Business Park, Inverness IV2 7GF. 01463 234171. www.hie.co.uk

Tourism Innovations Group, Scottish Tourism Forum, 29 Drumsheugh
  Gardens, Edinburgh EH3 7RN, 0131 220 6321.
  www.scotexchange.net/tig

Federation of Small Businesses, Scottish Office, 74 Berkeley Street,
  Glasgow G3 7DS. 0141 221 0775. www.fsb.org.uk

The Tourism Society Scotland, The Tourism Society, c/o Napier
  University, School of Marketing and Tourism, Craighouse Road,
  Edinburgh EH10 5LG. Fax: 0131 455 6269. www.tourismsociety.org

Scottish Tourism Forum, 29 Drumsheugh Gardens, Edinburgh EH3
  7RN. 0131 220 6321. www.stforum.co.uk

Self catering associations

The Association of Scotland's Self-Caterers, ASSC Secretary, Airdeny
  Chalets, Glen Lonan, Argyll PA35 1HY. 01866 822122.
  secretary@assc.co.uk www.assc.co.uk

Tourism in Northern Ireland

Regional tourism organisations

Derry Visitor and Convention Bureau, 44 Foyle Street, Derry BT48
6AT. +44 (0) 28 7137 7577. www.derryvisitor.com

Kingdoms of Down, 40 West Street, Newtownards BT23 4EN. +44 (0)
91 822 881. www.kingdomsofdown.com

Causeway Coast and Glens, 11 Lodge Road, Coleraine BT52 1LU.
+44 (0) 28 7032 7720. www.causewaycoastandglens.com

Belfast Visitor and Convention Centre, 47 Donegall Place, Belfast BT1
5AD. +44 (0) 28 9024 6609. www.gotobelfast.com

Fermanagh Lakeland Tourism, Wellington Road, Enniskillen BT74
7EF. +44 (0) 28 66 346 736. www fermanaghlakelands.com

Sperrins Tourism, 30 High Street, Moneymore, Co Londonderry BT45
7PD. +44 (0) 28 8674 7700. www.sperrinstourism.com

Government bodies associated with tourism

Invest NI, 64 Chichester Street, Belfast BT1 4JX. +44 (0) 28 9023
9090. www.investni.com

Department of Enterprise, Trade and Investment
+44 (0) 9052 9900
www.detini.gov.uk

Self catering organisations and associations

Rural Cottage Holidays
www.cottagesinireland.com and www.ruralcottageholidays.com

NI Self Catering Holidays Association (NISCHA)
+44 (0) 28 90 776174
www.nischa.com

Tourism statistics

Statistics and research on tourism.

www.staruk.org.uk

This is the official website of the UK Research Liaison Group made up of representatives from the National Tourist Boards of Britain, England, Wales, Scotland and Northern Ireland and from the Department for Culture, Media and Sport.

Also see national tourism websites:
England: www.tourismtrade.org.uk
Wales: www.wtbonline.gov.uk
Scotland: www.scotexchange.net
Northern Ireland: www.nitb.com

Quality Assurance

Details of the quality assurance schemes, including those for walkers and cyclists, the environment and accessibility, can be found on the national tourist industry websites.

England: www.tourismtrade.org.uk
Wales: www.wtbonline.gov.uk
Scotland: www.scotexchange.net
Northern Ireland: www.nitb.com

Green Schemes

In addition to the above websites, details of 'green tourism' can be found on the following websites.

England
For information on the Green Advantage Scheme contact:
www.welcometoexcellence.co.uk/green

Wales
For enquiries about the Green Dragon Standard contact:
ARENA Network, Wales Business Environment Centre, Main Avenue, Treforest Industrial Estate, Treforest, Pontypridd CF37

5UR. 01443 844001. Fax: 01443 844002. info@arenanetwork.org
www.arenanetwork.org

Every company achieving a Green Dragon Standard is featured on this
website: www.greendragonwales.com

Scotland

For enquiries about the Green Tourism Business scheme contact:
Green Tourism Business Scheme, Perth Business Centre, 28
Glasgow Road, Perth PH2 0NX. 01738 632162. Fax: 01738 622268
gtbs@green-business.co.uk
www.green-business.co.uk

Tourism and the Environment Forum, Thistle House, Beechwood Park
North, Inverness IV2 3ED. 01463 723 012.
www.greentourism.org.uk

Index

access to properties, 67–68, 69
advertising, 166–176
agencies, 164–165, 270
apartments, 51–53

bathrooms, 66, 81, 91–93, 119
bedrooms, 65–66, 80–81, 93–94, 118, 222
booking – on line, 187
booking forms, 180–182
bookings, 185–187
book keeping, 191–192
brochures, 173–174, 265–266
building/conversion, 64–74, 261–262
business cards and stationery, 174–175
business options, 19–23
business plans, 100–106
business rates, 246–248
by the sea, 40–41

cancellations, 181, 189–190
carbon monoxide detectors, 229
cash book, 192–194
cash flow, 106–108
chalets and lodges, 55–58
city or town living, 38–40
cleaning, end of visit, 216–218

cleaning, long term, 218–219
cleanliness, 117–118
common standards (QA), 117–120
complaints, 211–212
couples, 30–31

damp proofing, 72–73
Data Protection Act, 236–237
dealing with a death, 235
dealing with the guests, 199–202
decorating styles, 88–89
disability legislation, 74
Disability Schemes, 135–139
    England, 137
    Northern Ireland, 139
    Scotland, 138–139
    Wales, 137–138

E-Commerce Regulations, 234–235
electrical safety, 230–232
enquiries, 183–185
equipping the cottages, 79–84
establishing a workspace, 242

family holidays, 2, 29–30
fire extinguishers/fire blankets, 228

fire proofing, 71, 72
furniture – fire regulations, 229–230

gardens, 69–70, 222
gas safety regulations, 230
grants, 109–110
Green Schemes, 128–132, 267
   England, 130
   Northern Ireland, 131–132
   Scotland, 131
   Wales, 131
group holidays, 3, 31–32
guest information, 204–205
guest records, 190–191

halls and stairways, 94, 118
health and safety, 233
heating and hot water, 70–71, 232
holidays – personal, 258

insurance, 189–190, 236
in the countryside, 41–44

keeping motivated, 257–260
kitchens, 81–84, 90–91, 119

large house letting, 54–55
limited company, 248–249

magazine advertising, 171–173, 265
management efficiency, 118
methods of payment, 187–189
migrant workers, 234

multiple cottage letting business, 53–54

near main attractions, 44–45
newspaper advertising, 171, 265
Northern Ireland Tourist Board, 116, 122–124

office technology, 245–246
outdoor pursuits, 3
outside lighting, 74
outside maintenance, 222–224
overseas tourists, 27–28

painting and decorating, 219–220
personal profile, 16–19
planning permission, 63–64
pricing, 269
private water supplies and sewerage, 73–74, 223–224, 232–233
pro forma letters, 182
providing extras, 203–204

Quality Assurance, 117–124
questionnaires, 209–211, 269

refurbishment, 260–261
renewing furniture, 220–222
romantic breaks, 34
room dimensions, 67
room layout, 68
running workshops and courses, 262–263

setting up an office, 242–246
setting up the business, 12–16
short breaks, 270
sitting/dining rooms, 79–80, 94–96, 118, 221
single cottage letting business, 50–51, 247
small business rate relief, 247–248
smoke detectors, 228–229
sole trader/partnership, 249
social life, 259
sound proofing, 72
Standard Minimum Wage, 233–234

taking an 'away day', 258–259
taste, 90
tax and National Insurance, 248–249
terms and conditions, 180–182
tourist boards, 175–176
tourism organisations
    England, 144–147
    Northern Ireland, 155-158
    Scotland, 151–155

UK-wide, 144
Wales, 147–151

up-market holidays, 3, 33, 58–59, 266–267

VAT, 250–252
ventilation, 68–69
views from properties, 69
VisitBritain, 114–115, 120
VisitScotland, 116, 122

Wales Tourist Board, 115, 121
walkers and climbers, 28–29
Walkers and Cyclists Welcome Schemes, 132–135
    England, 132–133
    Northern Ireland, 135
    Scotland, 134–135
    Wales, 133–134
website
    commercial, 169–170, 265
    individual, 167–169, 265–266
weekenders, 32–33
welcome pack, 203
white goods, 221